AF540493

Challenges of the Twenty First Century

About the Author

Prof. P. Moorthy has inter-disciplinary Post-Graduate Degree Course, M.Sc (Peace-Making) from Madurai Kamaraj University and M.Phil. and Ph.D. (Disarmament Studies) from Jawaharlal Nehru University (JNU). He had research trip to United States (US), United Kingdom (UK), Nepal and Sri Lanka. He joined the newly started School of International Studies, Pondicherry University on 1 November 1988 and continued to serve the inter-disciplinary interest of the School. He is Founder Managing Director of Science and Technology for Knowledge Society and convener of "Mission Develop India Network Group". He has a number of publications to his credit including three books. He is an editorial fellow in three journals and visiting fellow of Shanti Peace Foundation, Coimbatore. He is also editor of a quarterly *Knowledge Society Journal* and has a number of awards and honours in recognition of his teaching and research profession. Recently, he was honoured with best citizen of India award.

Challenges of The Twenty First Century

P. Moorthy

CONCEPT PUBLISHING COMPANY PVT. LTD.
NEW DELHI-110059

ISBN-13-978-81-8069-702-9

First Published 2010

Published and Printed by

Concept Publishing Company Pvt. Ltd.
Regd. Office:
A/15-16, Commercial Block, Mohan Garden
New Delhi-110059 (India)
Phones : 25351460, 25351794, *Fax* : 091-11-25357109
Email : publishing@conceptpub.com,
website: www.conceptpub.com

Editorial Office:
H-13, Bali Nagar, New Delhi-110 015, India

Cataloging in Publication Data--*Courtesy:* D.K. Agencies (P) Ltd. <docinfo@dkagencies.com>

Moorthy, P. (Periakrishna), 1956-
Challenges of the twenty first century / P. Moorthy.
p. cm.
Includes bibliographical references and index.
ISBN 9788180697029

1. World politics--21st century. 2. Peace. 3. Security, International. 4. Nuclear weapons--Government policy--South Asia. 5. Terrorism--South Asia--Prevention. 6. Rural development--India. I. Title.

DDC 909 22

In the name of Allah, the most beneficent, the most merciful

Prof. **S.SATHIKH**, B.E. (Mech), M.E. (Design), Ph.D.
(Former Vice-Chancellor, University of Madras)

Ph. : (+91) (44) 24468734 Cell : (+91) 9444019734
E-mail : sathikh @ vsnl. net

Foreword

"Between greed and need and between the needless wants and the wantless needs lies the secret of Happiness"

It is with pleasure I pen this foreword to the book, *Challenges of the Twenty First Century*, authored by Prof. P. Moorthy. The choice of the very title is a challenge, since the author has ventured to fathom the unexplored depth of ocean of human issues of the days and the days to come. He has selected eight significant titles and attempted to present the issues, their implications and also some solutions, where possible.

The first two chapters are the focal points of what are elaborated in the chapters to follow. The subjects discussed are issues of world peace, global recession, its origin, what is in store, Gandhian alternative, views on modern economy, and toward a real economy. With all technologies, man has reduced his physical activities on useful productivity and is transforming from manual worker to knowledge worker, in Peter F. Drucker's words. This has resulted in lazy leisure nonproductive activities, unwanted thoughts and sickened body, as the old saying goes, the idle mind the devil's workshop. This leads the author to deliberate on Gandhian philosophy of economics, especially for less developed and developing nations. The interpretation of development indexed by GNP itself is contradictory to the concept of Gandhiji. GNP is a measure of *average*, which can be the same for 1 and 99; and 49 and 51. This is the paradox that haunts India now; with the majority struggling in poverty and a few enjoying the world's top ten positions among the richest. On the need for redefinition of development index, the UN has formulated a Human Development Index, including nutrition, health, education, human rights etc., reflecting the quality of life than simple material possessions. In the light of such index India unfortunately ranks very low. Yet the phenomenon of the rich becoming richer and the poor becoming poorer continues in India and elsewhere. This may be due to blind following of the western pattern by the developing countries, without properly modifying the same to suit their prevailing culture and socio-economic situations.

Recently a retired high ranking American officer cautioned India not to follow western consumerism that tempts people to buy needless things. A visiting ESCAP expert too cautioned India of its blind speedy development of the infrastructure, without training the manpower in the same pace to handle it, since it may end up in imbalance, again leading to poor becoming poorer and rich richer. The youth thrown unemployed in this process would become frustrated and end up in choosing one of the four options available: beg or steal or suicide or turn to terrorism.

All these are already happening. If the same course of consumerism that forces people to buy needless things at large, it would only intensify the problems. The solutions to all these are in the Gandhian approach, the author believes.

The World Peace is dealt elaborately with the implications emanating from economical, racial, religious, ideological and political differences. Conflicts are said to emerge from mismatch in objective, goal, role, style and value among the parties involved. Especially values may be different for different culture. What is good for one need not be so for others. Great understanding and adjustment, therefore, are needed to get harmony in all these factors. Again Gandhian concept finds a role here, in the sense and importance of respect to individuals, non-violence, *ahimsa*, *satyagraha*, etc. In recent times, people all over the world in general and national and international leaders in particular have started turning to Gandhian principles for refuge and salvation.

In the other chapters the author deals with nuclear, terrorism, human rights, rural India, disaster management and human rights. The author is point blank to expose some big powers who indulge in creating imbalance and causing injustice to the world community.

One could apply Gandhian approach for almost all issues that are listed in this book. Happiness comes from the achievement of what was aspired. When there is a gap between them, the smaller the gap, the greater is the happiness. Gandhiji said that for those who cannot achieve what was their aspiration, they only should lower their expectation to narow the gap and increase the happiness. It is pragmatic. It does not mean, however, one should not aspire high. But it implies that balanced growth should be aimed rather than lopsided. A lopsided growth leads to unhappiness. The happiness is a good yardstick of development, that represents, to some extent, the quality of life of the locals, though not an absolute quality. Gandhiji's simple terms are need and greed, the latter upsets, be it economy, peace or any other issues considered as challenges of the twenty-first century.

On the whole Prof. P. Moorthy has brought a book of food for thought, for all those who are worried about the future of this pleasant earth, perhaps of planets beyond in the universe, particularly for the researchers in these areas. He deserves compliments for this useful contribution of knowledge to the field of international affairs.

Preface

"Research carried in the rich countries on the problems of underdeveloped countries...tends to become "diplomatic", forbearing and generally overoptimistic"

—*Gunnar Myrdal*

Theory of *deterrence* that has proliferated continuous production, deployment and stockpiling of Weapons of Mass Destruction (WMD) amazingly wasting both human and material resources during the period of cold war and running counter to human development for almost five decades by forcing economic as well as human poverty on the face of the earth, has become obsolete today. As of the reason, the 'human development theory' is gaining in this new millennium. In this connection, the United Nations (UN) has declared the first decade of this century as culture of peace decade for achieving an alternative model based on 'non-violence' in addition to the historic declaration of 'Millennium Development Goals' (MDG) for eradicating extreme poverty by 2015.

Hundreds of nations, endorsing the MDG have been working towards this direction. Vision oriented plans with time bound missions are becoming, therefore, very popular in most of the developing countries. Countries of Africa, Asia and Latin America have been working on these human development agenda since 2000. India envisions for achieving a developed nation status by 2020, for which the Planning Commission has created a task force. Against this background, this book aims at evaluating pertinent issues of the world community to be resolved in this new millennium with the intention of attaining a new world order based on non-violent methods. For this purpose, it is divided into eight chapters. The first chapter introduces the issues of world peace in general and the second deals with nuclear issues of South Asia. The third chapter considers the task of combating global terrorism, while the fourth concentrates on issues of human rights. The fifth chapter is concerned with issues relating to the task of transforming rural India. The latest problems with regard to disaster management is studied by dealing with the case of 'tsunami' that occurred on 26th December, 2004 in the sixth chapter. The seventh chapter highlights the emerging areas of global peace and knowledge economy apart from highlighting the information technology and its connection for peace, prosperity and human development. The last chapter aims at finding solutions for the present global recession.

I thank all who have encouraged me for publishing this modest book, which is dedicated to the 'National Movement for Counselling the Youth', under the banner of 'Mission Develop India Network' as an offspring of Science and Technology for Knowledge Society inaugurated by the former Education Minister of Pondicherry Shri Lakshmi Narayanan and patronised by Dr. A.P.J. Abdul Kalam, the former President of India.

P. moorthy

Introduction

The book, *Challenges of the Twenty First Century* consists of eight chapters— world peace, South Asia's nuclear proliferation, terrorism in South Asia, human rights, rural India, disaster management, human development and knowledge economy and global recession. The first chapter is divided into three sections. Section one titled 'perennial problems' deals with three important issues—hunger, migration and alienation. It notes that the world population has crossed the mark of six billion already and it would cross the mark of nine billion in the next fifty years. Thus, it notes that two billion people are suffering from hunger and the majority of them are from Africa, Asia and Latin America.

The second issue—migration, which is yet another perennial problem to the human kind is dealt in the subsequent subsection that notes: "According to the United Nations, the world refugee population reached 45 million in 2000 and the UN Conventions on Refugees (UNCR) established in 1951 has been working tirelessly for facilitating these people. It helps people who are feared of being persecuted for reasons of race, religion, nationality, membership of a particular social group or political opinion. Also, those people who escape from famine, loss of means for feeding their children by natural disasters are helped by UNCR.... There are about 10 to 12 million people belonging to this category."

The third in this series is alienation. Alienation as a concept, is very ambiguous. However, for the purpose of this study, the following definition is considered in this section. It reads: " It is a state of mind of people who feel no affinity for their environment, perceive society as being hostile or indifferent to their existent and are convinced that no matter what they say or do no ones else care". According to the study, alienation is rooted primarily in poverty, backwardness, illiteracy and ill-health and half of the world population lives in such condition due to economic, political and social reasons. Most of them are living, as noted, in Africa, Asia and Latin America. Followed by alienation, poverty is discussed in this section, which points out that more than 27.9 per cent of the world population faces such problem altogether and more than 350 million people are living in poverty along with 118 million in extreme poverty.

Issues relating to the 'fabricated problems' are dealt in the next section. They are as follows: terrorism, new nuclear war of the US, regional wars, global corruption, education and conclusion. Terrorists in the world, violating all norms set forth by nation states as well as the global community like UN, are creating more problems to the already troubled world of today. Thousands of such organizations, big and small, working in explicit and implicit are collaborating with various miscreants those who work against peace among nations. The attack on World Trade Center (WTC) of the US by the Arab terrorists is the extreme and new form of human terrorism, which caused the life of twenty thousand people. Such terrorist acts are systematically studied in this section.

The next issue dealt in this section is the new nuclear threat. It exposes that the nuclear weapons are posing greater danger than any other threats and although they were the products of 1940s, still the world nations fascinate producing new types of weapons. It notes further that there were more than 70,000 nuclear weapons with the US and with the former Soviet Union during the period of the cold war 1945 to 1991. Even after signing various nuclear arms control treaties there are more than 22,000 thousand nuclear weapons with the US and Russia at present.

It continues that Russia, Ukraine, Belarus, and Kazakhstan are also planning to improve their nuclear weapon capability especially relating to the infrastructure to carry out effective war in the twenty first century. As mentioned above, there are now more than 22,000 such weapons, equal to 50,000 Hiroshima. A technically well-equipped nuclear missile called MX (missile experimental) can reach any part of the world in less than thirty minutes. The new nuclear weapon countries, India, Pakistan, and some other capable countries like Israel, North Korea, Argentina and Brazil are also having ambitious plans to produce and deploy such weapons in the future.

The problems of regional wars are studied in the subsequent subsection which evaluates the war scenarios in different regions of the world, especially in Africa, Asia and Middle East. According to it, until the end of the cold war, there were about fourteen full-scale wars and several major armed conflicts due to civil, economic and religious differences. Especially Europe, South America and Africa were the worst affected regions in this respect and, as per the study; in Africa alone 1.7 million people had lost their lives. Afghanistan, Colombia, Chechnya, Indonesia, Peru are the countries, as noted, facing severe wars within groups of people and the interstate wars leading to regional one occur due to the rouge behaviours of many nations in the world like Iraq, Israel, Turkey, Indonesia, North Korea, and Sudan.

Followed by the nuclear threat, the global corruption, as an important issue of the present world, is considered in this section. It notes that since the beginning of the day when man started worshipping idols, corruption has been there in the society and people have been fighting against it. Religious leaders responsible for the very formation of religions fought themselves and failed in avoiding corrupt practices in the idol worships that is one of the front-runners of corruption. For instance, it emphasizes that the great holy personalities like Isaiah, Buddha, Jesus and Muhammad who fought against the idol worship failed miserably and dishonesty spoils the younger generations even by forcing them to consume narcotic. According to it, such drugs are trafficked from different countries and dispatched to both developed and developing countries. The drugs from South East Asia reaches through many third world countries like India and Pakistan to both developed and developing countries such as US, UK, German, Russia, Brazil, Argentina.

Finally the educational necessities for avoiding all the issues referred in this section are highlighted beginning with Swami Vivekananda's statement: "to build up the manhood and womanhood of our world, education was a source of energy which can raise the world communities and get them gain their last individuality, human worth and dignity". Education, being the nerve centre for human development, as per the study, the value based educational movements by building global peace and knowledge society are pertinent to face all the challenges of the present century and it specifies that India should take lead since it aims at fostering international peace through its Article 51 of the Constitution.

The second chapter highlights the nuclear issues of South Asia, which consists of five sections. The techniques of nuclear technology and its process are dealt by the first and second section respectively and the third focuses on the nuclear activities of South Asia. The fourth and fifth sections study about the nuclear interest of India and Pakistan while the sixth and seventh about the critical lessons to be learned from the nuclear explosions and the recent developments in this region. The new nuclear order—proliferation security initiative (PSI) — is critically analyzed in the eighth section, which elaborates the historical aspect for managing nuclear energy crisis of the world and the American initiatives. The last section focuses on the role of the Pakistani scientist, A.Q. Khan and the impact. In conclusion, it suggests that since India and Pakistan have become nuclear weapon powers and more than seventy five per cent of the world thorium resource, as noted above, is located in India, the South Asia has strategic advantage in the future of world economy.

Therefore, managing energy as well as political crisis between nations in the region is becoming very important issues of the world community. Nuclear energy, though being used in this region for weapon purposes, comparatively it is not posing greater danger as India and Pakistan have declared their interests for minimum deterrent. In the constructive side of the energy, both of them are not too ambitious, as they have no such plans for producing huge energy based on nuclear sources. Thus, the management of nuclear energy, both destructive and constructive, lies in the hands of world community, which would possibly establish in this decade of the new millennium a 'new order for nuclear energy security' in a comprehensive way encompassing issues relating to all the regions of the world including South Asia.

The third chapter analyses the issue of terrorism with reference to South Asia, which is one of the major victims to the nexus of international terrorism. It runs into five sections: concept and history, the case of India, the post September 11 incidents, the impact of terrorism, non-zero sum game, the game of Pakistan, old politics in the new world and conclusion. It suggests that effective collision arrangement against international terrorism should be formed to eradicate terrorism as such.

The issues of human rights are studied in the fourth chapter under various subsections titled: history of human rights, critical analysis of the concept, human rights violation, woman and human rights, the plight of women in India, poverty and human rights. In conclusion, it is suggested that HR activists all over the world have to work together and consolidate the peace movements as a whole. They should not fall prey to politics or any other stakes. Forgetting about the differences, all countries of the world should help the activists by providing sufficient funds in order to help the helpless poor people.

All the activists involved in promoting HR should play, therefore, positive role without confusion especially on understanding the very concept. Women and children of the world have to be considered by the activists first and they should be helped with conviction. It notes further that activities in Africa, Asia, Latin America and other deserving regions of the world have to be intensified and more importantly, they should effectively utilize information and communication technology (ICT) for promotion of human rights in a faster phase.

Transforming rural India has become an important issue, which is deliberated in the fifth chapter. It consists of six sections: introduction, conceptual explanation, vision-2020, achieving 'PURA', knowledge revolution in rural India and conclusion with suggestion. It effectively argues for advancing the progress of rural India in this new millennium, as India is considered to be one of the important players for attaining international peace. It notes in its concluding remarks that to make India a developed nation, immediate attention has to be drawn for increasing the percentage of higher education from six per cent to thirty per cent by empowering the existing uiversities and by establishing new universtities in the coming years.

Both agricultural and educational fields can transform rural India more efficiently than any other fields. Such transformation will pave the way for a developed India in the future. Therefore, as noted, the new secular government led by Congress-I has to work not only for accelerating emoployment, growth and investment but also for providing social harmony, peace and 'purposeful knowledge' infrastructure. Such works of the government with vision, according to the study, would transform the rural India and promote the welfare of the farmers, farm labourers, youths, women and weaker sections.

The sixth chapter discusses about issues relating to disaster management. It is divided into seven sections as follows: introduction, understanding the origin of disaster, the earthquake, tsunami and the Indian experiences, disaster warning system and concdsion. It suggests that Disaster management has become one of the important areas of studies in this present century. As Indian Ocean is the most vulnerable region to such natural disasters including earthquakes and tsunamis, apart from being vulnerable to droughts, floods, cyclones, landslides and bush fires, the task for establishing disaster management network has become very significant one in this part of the globe.

Therefore, Indian Ocean countries should continue to work for establishing effective early warning system in the tsunami-genic places like Java, Sumatra and Makaram For the purpose, they should tirelessly work for establishing links with gigantic communication network of the world community available with more than seventy-five nations now irrespective of politics and cultural differences. Such 'global network' may help, as noted in this chapter, the scientists for advancing further in this field especially in predicting the 'primary pulse' of the earthquakes in the future.

The issues in realation to human development and knowledge economy are dealt in the seventh chapter under six sections: the dawn of 'knowledge age', managing the economy—the foundation for technological society, silicon valley—the way for knowledge economy, peace through information technology and the knowledge society, importance of knowledge management and conclusion. It suggests in conclusion that for achieving human development and knowledge economy, which will support the avowed interest for building global peace, it is pertinent to build on knowledge society based on new 'social order of equanimity' contributing to develop a new civilization and culture that can help establish not only economically prosperous nations but also politically cohesive world. It advocates that the global knowledge society and national development are part and parcel and it can be achieved by implementing all the technological means including the information technology at all levels especially giving utmost considerations for the present liberalized economic system of the world nations.

The last chapter aptly focuses on the latest issues of global recession. It starts with the quotation of Mahatma Gandhi: "... this (human) body is a most delicate piece of machinery... The spinning wheel is a machine; a little toothpick is a machine. What I object to is the craze for machinery not machinery as such. The craze is for what they call labour-saving machinery. Men go on 'saving labour' till thousands are without work and thrown on the open streets to die of starvation. I want to save time and labour not for a fraction of mankind but for all. I want the concentration of wealth, not in the hands of a few, but in the hands of all". It also notes that the present economic crisis is due to the misconduct of American economy and, therefore, it should be managed by adopting the *swaraj* perspectives of Mahatma Gandhi. For the purpose, it is divided into six sections. The first section deals with the origin of the world economic crisis and the second with present global recession.

The third section focuses on the lessons of Gandhiji with reference to *Hind Swaraj*. New methods for resolving present crisis and the failure of the modern economic paradigm are analyzed in the fourth and fifth section respectively. The sixth section highlights the importance of developing 'real economy'—the economy of the 'poorest of the poors' in the context to India and the last section conculdes with suggestions for erecting new economic order by replacing the Bretton Woods System, which was formed in 1944. Hence, the book explores new avenues with an interest for managing the challenges of the twenty first century.

Contents

Chapter -1

Issues of World Peace

Introduction

The international community is faced with a number of tribulations in this new millennium. Although all the religious philosophies of the world advocate for peace and harmony, they are not being implemented because of the attrition of human values. Therefore, conflicts among nations have been in rapid increase. Since the beginning of the formation of nation states through Westphalia Treaty signed in 1648, thousands of wars were fought by the world nations causing a loss of more than a billion lives.[1] India alone had lost two million people due to religious conflicts after 1947. Besides, millions of people die every year due to starvation in Africa, Latin America and in Asia. The West African countries are the worst affected in this respect. The poverty situation has been fast engulfing even in the oil-rich countries of the Middle East due to continuous American wars since the late 1980s.

The American interest for warin Middle East nations is based on their philosophy that Iran, Iraq and North Korea are the 'Axis of Evil' and they will threaten not only the security of US but also the entire world. As the US has taken a similar, but proxy war, position with the former Soviet Union during the period of cold war advocating that the Soviet Union was a 'Evil Empire' and, therefore, it should be fought. Such war went ahead until 1991, the year when the demise of Soviet Union took place.[2] As planned by the Americans, the conduct of foreign policy by war in Middle East is likely to continue until the fall of 'Axis of Evil.'

Apart from deliberate wars, terrorism (the concept is not yet defined) in different parts of the world causes concern, as it let lose mindless violence on innocent people of the world. India has lost more than seventy thousand people including two Prime Ministers. The international terrorist network is powerful, as it has rocked the mind of the Americans specifically after the September 11, 2001 incident. The nexus is, therefore, to be fought collectively. Nevertheless, the Americans, as they have their own national agenda for promoting their interest not bothering for the common good or bothering for their own brand of common good, go alone or dominate in dealing with the global terrorism by skipping even the direction of the UN.[3] In this connection, many argue that the objectives of American war on Afghanistan and Iraq are defeated particularly since they did not succeed either in catching up Bin Laden in Afghanistan or Weapons of Mass Destruction (WMD) in Iraq.

For such unilateral measure, the US spends more than seventy per cent of its budget on military build up including Research and Development (R&D). There are already thousands of nuclear weapons available in American inventory that spreads not only economic burden but also the psychological one among world nations. As a result, countries not affordable are forced to spend extravagantly on military depriving the human development. There are about eighty such countries in this psychosomatic syndrome having stockpiled WMD including nuclear, chemical and biological weapons.[4] India and Pakistan are also in this quagmire.

Perennial Problems—Hunger

The world population has crossed the mark of six billions already and it would cross, as predicted, about nine billions in the next fifty years. Apart from this problem what one calls as 'population explosion', the present world will also face number of other problems due to lack of human values, which have to be dealt with carefully by effective ways by adopting various techniques available in the world especially in the area of science and technology such as information technology (IT). Despite of the efforts taken over the period since 1945, the year when the UN was formed, the problems have been persistent until today.

Hunger has been one of the protracting problems of the world community from the very beginning of the human life. From the eighteenth century onwards, people have been working for eradicating poverty in the world. For instance, the British political economist, Thomas Malthus, cautioned the mankind with alarm pointing out that the world food supply would continue growing at an arithmetic rate and the population would grow at a much faster geometric or exponential rate. Despite, it has been persisting until today. Millions of people in Africa, Asia and Latin America have been suffering from hunger.

In Asian countries alone more than three millions of people go to bed without supper, five millions work in the fields without lunch, more than five million babies are fed only once in a day and more than two million youths ranging from the age group between eighteen and twenty-seven die every year due to hunger. In Asian countries, it has been persisting from the ancient time itself. For example, in one of the Chinese literature, it is pointed out that hunger was the father of invention not only in China but also in most countries of Asia. References were also made in Indian literature with regard to the impact of hunger.[5] For instance, a well-known poet in Tamil, Subramanian Bharathiyar, who was a freedom fighter, pointed out in his poem that "if a person does not have food, let us destroy the world." The most important and thought provoking speech was made in this respect by the great saint of the twentieth century Swami Vivekananda who noted that "so long as the millions live in hunger and ignorance, I hold every man a traitor who, having been educated at their expense, pays not the least heed to them".[6]

The problem of hunger is expanding even in the present world, as the affluent countries are following self-centered opportunistic policies. Therefore, the inequitable system of distribution exists, which does not help the developing countries despite the efforts taken by the United Nations and its related organizations. The poor people of the developing countries, especially in Africa, Asia and Latin America, are in great trouble to this perennial problem. Chronically undernourished people by region are as follows in millions: Asia (500), Africa (190), Latin America (50), Middle East (30), Russia/E. Europe (30). Thus, totalling together 800 million people are in need of help. As of the reason, hunger death is ever increasing in these regions. Although the excess agricultural production is recorded overall, the developing countries are deprived from getting enough foodgrain to supply to the needy people. The world as a whole has, as noted by the World Development Report, more than two billion people living under poverty line.[7] The UN Millennium Goal of 2000 approved by 189 countries aims at eradicating extreme poverty in the world by 2015 and planned to achieve hunger-free world by 2007 which could not be attained even today.

Migrants

Yet another problem perennial to the humankind in the world is related to migration and immigration of people. According to the report of the UN the world refugee population reached 46 millions in 2000.[8] The UN Conventions on Refugees (UNCR) established in 1951 has been working tirelessly for facilitating these people. It helps people who are feared of being persecuted for reasons of race, religion, nationality, membership of a particular social group or political opinion. Also, people those who escape from famine, loss of means for feeding their children by natural disasters are helped by UNCR.[9] Immigrants in search of better life than the life they lead in their native countries are also extended help by the UNCR. There are about 10 to 12 million people belonging to this category.

In the recent time, with the added advantages of proliferation of information technology (IT), thousands of people from developing countries are interested to settle down in western countries by illegal means which increases the number of migrants in the world overall. For instance, reported news in the regional passport office in India can be noted. According to it, thousands of young people ageing from 21 to 27 are desperate to go out of country by illegal means, especially to settle down in US, by making false certifications as if they have been educated and trained in IT areas.[10] Increasing unemployment is also one of the reasons why the youths are driven to adopt such illegal means. According to International Labour Organization (ILO), global youth unemployment amounts to 180 million. Since 1995, it has been growing in the regions like Latin America, Caribbean, Middle East and North African countries. In Middle East and North Africa, there are about 26 per cent of the youth population remaining unemployed. Sub-Saharan Africa, although improved in recent time, has 18 per cent of its population unemployed.

Alienation

Alienation, as a concept, is very ambiguous. However, for the purpose of this study, the following definition can be considered: "It is a state of mind of people who feel no affinity for their environment, perceive society as being hostile or indifferent to their existent and are convinced that no matter what they say or do no ones else care".[11] Although there are differences of opinion about the causes of alienations, it is accepted by many scholars that alienation is rooted primarily in poverty, backwardness, illiteracy, ill-health and in general in conscious perceptions of social, economic, and political inequality. According to one report, half of the world population lives in such condition due to economic, political and social reasons. Most of them are living in Africa, Asia and Latin America. Even in the developed countries also such problems prevail.[12] For instance, in United States the majority of the black people suffer from such alienation and in the European countries too such problems prevail. As a result, people live in pathetic condition.

Poverty

Poverty has been worst spread all over the world as people living on less than one dollar per day are increasing in number. More than 27.9 per cent of the world population faces such problem altogether and more than 350 million people are living in poverty and 118 million in extreme poverty. Although the reduction level is fast picking up in Asian countries, it is not encouraging in African and Latin American countries. Poverty levels in Europe and Central Asia are also not showing the symptom of improvement despite changes in their economic approaches. It is reported, as usual in many other cases, the Sub-Saharan Africa is leading in poverty where more than 314 million people continue to live on less than one dollar a day. The Middle East and North Africa are also having more number of poverty-ridden people. People living under poverty line are more in South Asia. In India alone, there are 220 million people. However, Sub-Saharan Africa leads in possession of sizable proportion more than South Asian countries. According to recent data, more than a billion live on less than one dollar a day. As result, a minimum standard of living for them is in distant dream. It is also estimated that there are 2.73 billion people live on less than two dollars a day. Among them, more than half of the population lives in the developing world. The numbers living on less than two dollars a day will continue to rise in the Middle East and North Africa and Sub-Saharan Africa. In East Asia, the situation is better.

Poverty, as every one agrees, occurs mainly by uneven distribution of the world resources in general and surplus accumulation of wealth by individuals. Because of these reasons, the problem relating to human security—job security, income security, health security, environmental security and security from crime has become a routine one. Such problems impose certain illegal economic activities among people.[13] For example, the spread of forced prostitution affecting millions of young girls all over the world, especially in the developing countries, can be noted. Moreover, disabled people constituting ten per cent of the world's populations are living without having basic amenities because of such syndrome. The forced child labours numbering more than 250 million children are not given with educational facilities at all. For example, in India millions of children are involved in economic activities. A report states that more than 62 per cent of the children in the socially backward communities have never visited school in their life. The trend in the health condition of the people of the world is also very bad, as the spread of diseases is rampant due to malnutrition among children of the developing countries.[14]

Further, communicable, tropical, vaccine preventable, environmental, family, reproductive and non-communicable diseases are widespread in these countries. Apart from the spread of communicable diseases like cholera, dysentery hemorrhagic fever, hepatitis, meningitis, plague, rabies and zoo noses, HIV/AIDS are also found in some of the Asian and Latin American countries.[15] It is estimated that 40 million adults and 2.5 million children are living with HIV/AIDS and more than 98 of them in developing countries and 66 per cent in Sub-Saharan Africa. It is also noted that there are almost a million new cases in South and East Asia, where more than eight million people are now living with HIV/AIDS.

HIV/AIDS, tuberculosis, and malaria are killing maximum number of people in the world in general and in developing countries in particular. They affect not only the economy of the country but also the world economy as a whole. The economic impact in the LDC due to theses diseases is more severe than any other countries. Preventing such diseases can improve the economy of the respective countries and reduce overall poverty. For instance, tuberculosis costs the average patient three or four months of his or her earning and thus affects thirty per cent of individual income annually. In the case of Malaria, it is reported that it has already slowed down the economic growth of Africa by about 1.3 per cent a year. Similarly, HIV/AIDS affects eight per cent of the economic growth of the world in general. Prevention programmes are not reaching the deserving countries. Only one person affected by the disease out of five get the medical attention in the world.

The situation in the developing countries is even worst.

Comprehensive prevention measures are, therefore, needed. Otherwise, it will affect severely, as the thirty million new cases found at present are expected to reach the level of forty five million per year in the year, 2010. Five to six million people need HIV treatment in low- and middle-income countries, where only seven per cent of them get medical treatment. More than half of the newly infected people are between 15 and 24 years old. East Africa, Southern Africa, East Asia, the Pacific and the Middle East and North Africa are some of the regions badly affected in this respect. Education alone can help prevent this deadliest disease. In the case of Malaria, children are the worst affected groups. It is endemic in large parts of the developing world, particularly in tropical and subtropical regions, as it is not clinically diagnosed or reported for treatment. The World Health Organization (WHO) estimates that 300 to 500 million cases occur each year, leading to 1.1 million deaths. Almost 90 per cent of all cases occur in Sub-Saharan Africa, where children are the most affected.

Preventive measures for these diseases in developing countries are worst. If countries follow the way Vietnam could follow, the number of death incidents can be reduced. It is reported that more than16 per cent of children in Vietnam sleep under bed nets. By simply providing nets to all family can take care of preventing malaria in a considerable way. However, in Africa, only seven countries out of 27 use bed nets. All other countries are least bothered in providing such facilities to people especially to children. As a result, mortality rate reached 25 per cent in Africa. Further, tuberculosis kills around two million people a year. Most of the victims are between 15 to 45 years old. Each year there are about eight million new cases found. Among the new cases, around two million in Sub-Saharan Africa, three million in Southeast Asia, and more than a quarter million in Eastern Europe and the former Soviet Union are found. It is reported that out of 1,00,000 people, it affects 358. Sub-Saharan Africa is worst affected region in the world. Tuberculosis is also fast spreading in Europe and Central Asia.

The lowest rates are in Latin America, the Caribbean, the Middle East and North Africa. The following section focuses on terrorism.

Fabricated Problems—Terrorism

Apart from the above problems, many other fabricated problems confront the world community. Popular among such problems in this respect are terrorism, new nuclear war of the US, regional wars and global corruption. Terrorists in the world, violating all norms set forth by nation states as well as the global community like UN, are creating more troubles to the already troubled world of today. Thousands of such organizations, big and small, working in explicit and implicit are collaborating with various miscreants those who work against peace among nations.[16] The attack on World Trade Center (WTC) of the US by the Arab terrorists is the extreme and new form of human terrorism, which caused the life of twenty thousand people. Generally, the terrorists carry out their activities through various means including hijacking civilian airplanes and taking civilians into their custody. They demand ransom for returning the hostages or for returning their leaders who are arrested by the respective nations.

Yielding to such demands not only encourages them but also approve their activities as legal one. Therefore, Italy has enacted a law that prevents paying ransom to the terrorist. There was also incident in Colombia where the rebels blocked the roads demanding a huge amount of money from foreigners and rich locals. Similarly, in Nigeria, oil workers put in custody by terrorists with the expectation of more money for returning them.[17]

Iran, Sudan, Libya, North Korea, Cuba, Iraq and Syria generally support such terrorist activities. For example, since the year 1988 when Syria hijacked and bombed the American plane, the number of such hijacking increased in the world. There are several incidents occurred after 1988. The recent hijacking of Indian Airlines Airbus to Afghanistan from Nepal has drawn the attention of the world and helped initiate global action against such terrorism in 1999. In addition, immediate legal action was initiated for the first time in the history of taking action against such criminal activities. Culprits involved in the incidents were exposed within a short span of time, as the Sessions Judge, Mr. S.N. Aggarwal declared Ibrahim Akhtar, Shakil, Abdul Rauf, Yusuf Azhar, Sunny Ahmed Kazi, Jahur Ibrahim Mistri and Shahaid Sayid Akhtar as offenders.[18]

The cultural terrorism also threatens the world community today, as one looks at the way the Taliban's activities organized against the ancient and world popular Buddha's statues in Bamiyan region of Afghanistan. These statues were carved about 2000 years ago. Many nations of the world protested against this state-sponsored terrorism. Buddhist countries like Sri Lanka, Japan, China and some countries in the South East Asia have appealed the UN to take action against such activities that affect the sentiment of the Buddhist people of the world. This was also condemned by India from where Buddhism was originated. Pierre Lafrance of UNESCO, who met the Foreign Minister of Afghanistan, Mutta Wakil described the Taliban action against Bamiyan Buddha Statue as "crime against culture".[19] However, the Taliban did not listen to the appeal rather they went ahead destroying some more statues. Such trend in the world is more serious than ever before.

New Nuclear Threat

Nuclear weapons are posing greater danger than any other threats. Although they were the products of 1940s, still the world nations fascinate producing new types of weapons. Before dealing with the danger of nuclear weapons, some preliminary comments should be made in relation to the manufacture of nuclear weapons. Weapons-grade fissile material is the crucial ingredient for nuclear weapons. Production of plutonium-239 (Pu-239) by neutron bombardment of uranium-238 in a reactor, and enrichment of uranium to produce highly enriched uranium-235 (HEU), are the two most common methods of producing fissile material for bombs. (A third method is reactor irradiation of thorium to produce fissile uranium-233.) Production of plutonium requires a reactor—either a purpose-built reactor, a power reactor, or a research reactor—plus reprocessing facilities for extracting the plutonium from spent fuel. Reprocessing facilities can also be used to extract HEU or uranium-233 from irradiated material.

Uranium enrichment facilities are generally complex and expensive, but as methods of enrichment have been developed and improved, the potential for production of HEU bombs has increased. In nearly all countries pursuing nuclear weapons programmes, efforts have been made to domestically produce plutonium and/or to enrich uranium, but it is also possible to acquire weapons-grade fissile material by gift, theft, or purchase (including diversion of material acquired for civil purposes). In addition to fissile material, components such as high explosives, firing triggers, and handling devices are also required. Developing these components requires considerable technical skill, although producing or acquiring weapons-grade fissile material is the biggest obstacle. Some delivery systems, such as aircraft modified for delivery of nuclear weapons, pose no great obstacle, but advanced missile systems are far more complex and expensive.

There were more than 70,000 nuclear weapons with the US and with the former Soviet Union during the period of the cold war 1945 to 1991. It should be mentioned that whether cold war exists today or not is not the question to be addressed here. Even after signing various nuclear arms control treaties there are more than twenty thousand nuclear weapons with the US and Russia. Besides, huge amount of money is being spent on exploring the new nuclear weapons. For example, the US Department of Energy (DoE) has decided to launch a nuclear missile by the help of supercomputer. Russia, Ukraine, Belarus, and Kazakhstan are also planning to improve their nuclear weapon capability especially relating to the infrastructure to carry out effective war in the twenty first century.

The UK, France, China, India and Pakistan have been advancing their nuclear weapons systems including the thermonuclear fusion weapons, which are usually fuelled by isotopes of hydrogen and also require a nuclear fission detonator– as well as relatively advanced delivery systems. UK has more than hundred strategic nuclear as well as tactical weapons respectively. France is reportedly having for about five hundred strategic weapons. China's weapons are estimated to be more than five hundred. Its forces also include word tactical weapons. India and Pakistan have become nuclear weapon countries in the year 1998 and they were reported to be having number of nuclear weapons for delivery.

The spread of nuclear weapon technology is the yet another problem hunting the world community today. Israel has clandestinely developed between fifty to hundred nuclear weapons, and it has nuclear-capable ballistic missiles. France supported it in the beginning and now by the US. Word The Israeli nuclear weapons programme was launched in 1956, a year after the Chinese programme, which was started in 1957. Word Iran has been very seriously working to develop nuclear weapons since 1987, the year when its two research reactors were damaged by Iraqi air strikes and it has been reportedly involving in acquiring fabricated weapons from any country. Its programme is being supported by Russia, China and North Korea periodically. Iraq, being ardent enemy of the US in this region and which has faced two dangerous wars waged by the US and the UK in 1991 and in 2003, has been obviously interested to obtain or develop nuclear weapons. Since 1960s, it has been trying.

However, it obtained nuclear materials from former West Germany, Portugal, Niger, Brazil, Italy, France, Britain, and the Former Soviet Union. It has to be noted here that US bombing during the Gulf War in 1991 destroyed the nuclear facilities of Iraq. Libya has been trying to be capable in this field by connections with various countries such as China, countries of former Soviet Union, France, India, and Pakistan. Algeria is being supported by Argentina and China. Some more countries, which are ambitious in the region, if not for weapon capability, are Egypt, Syria, and Saudi Arabia.

North Korea is another potential country that has been involving in the field for quite some time. Various countries such as the former Soviet Union and China have supported its programme. Although it singed the NPT in 1985, it did not allow IAEA to inspect its nuclear facilities. It is also reported to be developing ICBM capability with the support of Egypt and Iran and to be trying to sell long-range missiles to Iran and Libya. Yet another country in this region trying to establish its presence felt in the nuclear field is South Korea that has been well supported by the US for so many years. Taiwan also has substantial nuclear weapon programme like South Korea. South Africa pursued a nuclear weapons programme and abandoned it later. Although it joined the NPT by 1991, it has been involving into nuclear activities. France had helped South Africa in the initial period.

Argentina had pursued a covert nuclear weapons programme for many years, refused to accede to the NPT, and did not sign the Treaty for the Prohibition of Nuclear Weapons in Latin America, popularly known as the Tlatelolco Treaty. Its nuclear programme was supported by Canada, West Germany, Switzerland and the Former Soviet Union. Brazil also pursued a covert nuclear weapons programme in response to Argentina's programme, which was supported by West Germany, France, and the US. Both Argentina and Brazil have ratified the Tlatelolco Treaty and agreed to IAEA inspections later. Romania, after ratifying the NPT in 1970, had involved in a covert activity to produce nuclear weapons. Sweden and former Yugoslavia had showed interest in this field by virtue of their being well connected with prominent nuclear states. Apart from these countries, number of other countries interested to develop nuclear weapons by being close to weapon states are: Australia, Austria, Belgium, Bulgaria, Canada, Chile, the Czech Republic, Denmark, Finland, Germany, Hungary, Indonesia, Ireland, Italy,

Japan, Mexico, the Netherlands, Norway, Poland, Slovakia, Slovenia, Sweden, Switzerland and Spain.

Due to the spread of nuclear technology, the threat of nuclear war is ever looming. Wars have been occurring from the beginning of the period of human settlements. Thousands of wars fought for acquiring more lands and properties killing more than billion people all over the world. Although there were no wars involving, major countries after the first and the second world wars, there were number of wars occurred in various regions annihilating millions of people. During the last fifty years, armed conflicts among nations of the world have claimed approximately twenty-seven million lives. It is estimated that civilians represent eighty five per cent of the casualties, with a majority being children and the elderly.[20] In the last decade alone, there occurred more than hundred wars in different regions of the world especially based on the religious differences. It is price worthy to know here that approximately eighty-three per cent of the world's population is adhered to some formal religious or spiritual belief system. Fearing to religious conflicts, majority of the people seek political asylum in different countries.

According to a recent report, more than four million people seek asylum every year in Europe due to fear of conflicts in their respective nations based on religious differences.[21] Since 1930s during the period when the "exodus of scientist" took place from Europe to United States in which Albert Einstein was one of the leading members, the refugee problem has been bothering the world nations. In addition, the problem relating to the misuse of refugees by the recipient countries are yet another problem that questions the very credibility of scientists. In this context, Einstein had lamented immediately after listening to the news of American bombing on Hiroshima on 6 August 1945 as follows: "had I known what disaster the bomb could do, I would have chosen to be single shoemaker of Switzerland rather than play any part in its (atomic weapons) creation".[22] Since 1945, thousands of nuclear weapons have been produced and deployed all over the world, as noted above. Some of the important events of nuclear era are mentioned below.[23]

- December 2, 1942: The Nuclear Age began at the University of Chicago when Enrico Fermi made a chain reaction in a pile of uranium;
- August 6, 1945: The United States dropped an atomic bomb on Hiroshima, Japan, killing over 100,000;
- August 9, 1945: The United States dropped an atomic bomb on Nagasaki, Japan, killing over 40,000;
- November 1, 1952: The first large version of the hydrogen bomb (thousands of times more powerful than the atomic bomb) was exploded by the United States for testing purposes; and
- February 21, 1956: The first major nuclear power plant opened in England.

There are now more than 22,000 such weapons, equal to 50,000 Hiroshima (the Japanese city wherein the American atomic bomb, 'little boy' was used killing several thousands of civilians) available even after signing many arms control agreements. A technically well-equipped nuclear missile called MX (missile experimental) can reach any part of the world in less than eighteen minutes and destroy 140 well-developed cities like Tokyo, Washington, Moscow, and London. There are about hundred MX missiles with US and equal versions are available with the present Russia. Moreover, there are also air launched and submarine launched ballistic missiles, which are in alert condition by nuclear weapon countries: US, Russia, United Kingdom, France and China. The new nuclear weapon countries, India, Pakistan, and some other capable countries like Israel, North Korea, Argentina and Brazil are having ambitious plans to produce and deploy such weapons in the future.[24] Therefore, of all the challenges, the threat of nuclear war remains as one of the major one. The world has witnessed, as noted above, verity of nuclear weapons deployed in the land, sea and in the outer space. The outer space nuclear arms are very much increasing in number today since many countries are interested in developing such arms. There are about thirty countries in the world having such nuclear potentials. The US, Russia, United Kingdom, France and China are leading in this field.[25]

Third world countries like India, Israel, Pakistan, Argentina, Brazil, North Korea, Iran and Iraq are fast developing this technology and some of them developed already their own indigenous missiles. Because of the third world's involvement, the Americans are planning to develop yet another system known as National Missile Defense (NMD) or Theatre Missile Defense (TMD) in order to defend their nation and their friendly countries in case of missile attack launched by any countries.[26] According to Americans, the third world country like Iraq and North Korea may plan for hitting the US by missiles. For avoiding such acts, the US already carried out NMD test by spending a huge amount of dollars. American plan of NMD has been under preparation since 1983.[27]

The arms control agreements relating to space based weapons such as Outer Space, and Anti-Ballistic Missiles (ABM) treaties are impractical as the US has developed plans for building space based military stations. Although the Russians are not interested unlike the US in developing similar system of NMD, the recent initiative for establishing defensive shield in Europe by Russia demonstrate that Russia is also considering the NMD type of Weapons and it is not sticking to the promises made in the ABM as well as in the Outer Space treaties.[28] Situation, therefore, is not very conducive now for controlling nuclear weapons.

Regional Wars

Yet another problem facing the globalizing world of twenty first century is the regional wars. Most of the third world countries have been facing such wars in different regions of the world, especially in Africa, Asia and Middle East. Until the end of the cold war, there were about fourteen full-scale wars and several major armed conflicts due to civil, economic and religious differences. Especially Europe, South America and Africa were the worst affected regions in this respect. For example in Africa, alone 1.7 million people had lost their lives because of regional wars.[29] As is the case with Angola, where more than million people have lost their lives and millions were displaced due to wars. In Algeria, battle between Muslim fundamentalists and the government forces have caused the lives of millions of people. In addition, in Sudan, the civil war that began in the year 1956 took the life of millions. Since 1984, fight has been going on in Turkey between Government and Kurdish minority people killing thousands of people. In India, such war has taken the life of forty thousand people since 1989.

Afghanistan, Colombia, Chechnya, Indonesia, Peru are the countries facing severe wars within groups of people. In addition, the inter-state wars leading to regional one occur due to the rouge behaviours of many nations in the world. For example, Iraq, Israel, Turkey, Indonesia, North Korea, and Sudan are responsible for regional tension in their respective regions. However, the definition of rouge state is debatable. Moreover, the inconsistent behaviours of the big power like the US causes tension among various regions. For instance, the former President Clinton declared openly in 1993 that the "US would behave and act multilaterally when possible and unilaterally when necessary".[30] This policy has been meticulously followed by the Administration since than.

Global Corruption

Corruption in the world is fast proliferating like an infectious disease. It is rocking the world communities in different fields. The word corruption is defined in the Oxford Dictionary as dishonesty, immorality or accepting bribes. All these practices exist in politics, societies and economics of the 'fast-track world' of today. It is in all levels and in all countries. More than illiterate people the so-called literate people are adopting it. It is in practice generally for quick and affluent economic development by a person or organization.[31] It has almost become a culture or system followed by generation after generation. Fighting against it has become so tuff today.

Since the beginning of the day when man started worshipping idols, corruption has been there in the society and people have been fighting against it. Religious leaders responsible for the very formation of religions themselves fought and failed in avoiding corrupt practices in the idol worships that is one of the front-runners of corruption For instance, the great holy personalities like Isaiah, Buddha, Jesus and Muhammad who fought against the idol worship failed miserably.[32] Even the teachings of these originators starting from the period, 805 B.C when Isaiah of Israel first preached against the idol worship could not prevent people having over ambition in taking advantages in such worships. Capitalizing for fast development in the economic front, therefore, had become the order of the day even in the ancient time, which continues even today.

Dishonesty has produced millions of corrupt people all over the world. From small village to the United Nations, which aims at establishing 'global village', one can encounter corrupt people. No countries in the world are exclusive of it. The affluent countries like US, Japan, France, Italy, Germany, and Switzerland are leading in this field. The present politicians of the world lead in corruption forgetting about the real philosophy of politics.[33] Immorality is the dominant factor that makes people involve in corruption even by using technology including the over emphasized information technology (IT). Thus, they are well equipped with 'digital eyes' for minting money. As a result, the educational sectors to be socially conscious and service oriented have become most corruptive. Thus, educational institutes all over the world from Primary schools to Universities have become the asylums of corruptive intellectuals and immoral activities.[34]

Dishonesty spoils the younger generations even by forcing them consume narcotic and killing capable drugs for the sake of making money. Such drugs are trafficked from different countries and dispatched to both developed and developing countries. The drugs from South East Asia reaches through many third world countries like India and Pakistan to both developed and developing countries such as US, UK, Germany, Russia, Brazil, Argentina respectively. The drug trafficking groups in the world also involve in different offensive activities including smuggling arms that concern for national security. According to the report by the former Admiral Vishnu Bhagwat of India, a coterie of drug smugglers are very active in the subcontinent and are responsible for overall smuggling of sizable numbers of arms and ammunitions in 1999 causing not only the embarrassment to India alone but also to many nations of the world.[35]

Obligation—The Educational Necessities

For resolving both the natural and fabricated problems highlighted in this article, only the 'positive education' to the entire humanity appears to be viable source. Such education, universal in nature, should provide all the value, knowledge and morality-based understanding on subjects of world importance including the issues discussed above. In the context to educational revival, Swami Vivekananda once referred that "to build up the manhood and womanhood of our world, education was a source of energy which can raise the world communities and get them gain their last individuality, human worth and dignity".[36] His proposition is true as one looks at the present world. Illiteracy is prevalent in the world that branded to be heading towards 'knowledge society'. African, Latin American, and Asian countries are crowded with the massive illiterate population.

Therefore, the huge amount allotted for construction of deadly weapons should be utilized for universal education, for which the United Nations should enact certain acts as it has recently done in the case of corruption. In this connection, the preamble of Universal Declaration of Human Rights (UDHR) states: "Education should be directed to the full development of the human personality and the strengthening of respect for human rights and fundamental freedoms. It shall promote understanding, tolerance and friendship among the nations, racial or religious groups, and shall further the activities of the United Nations for the maintenance of peace".[37]

Education, being the nerve centre for human development, has achieved certain objectives in helping out the developing world for overall economic developments. For example, primary health and family planning have reduced birth and death rates and increased life expectancy. They also helped in reducing infant mortality.[38] This trend in third world is due to the increased commitment to the development policies and the changes to the individual attitudes by education as such. Apart from solving these problems, education can also help eradicate poverty, which is centre of many problems of humankind. As per the artificial problems are concerned, it can play an interesting role by putting people to people contact as the motivating vehicle for international peace. Non Governmental Organizations (NGOs) can initiate by taking advantages of the latest technologies, especially the ICT, in order to educate the population of the entire world in coordination with many international agencies like UNESCO and WHO.

Conclusion

Value based educational movements by building global peace and knowledge societies are pertinent to face all the challenges of the present century. India should take lead since it aims at fostering international peace through its Article 51 of the Constitution. All nations should brawl for world democracy and equality by avoiding the narrow consideration of promoting national interest of their own. The over push of any one's national interest should be, therefore, regulated not depriving the majority of the poor and deserving countries. If not, no peace, neither economic nor political, would be viable and the uneven development would continue even if the world repeats thousands of globalization process. Therefore, the UN should help the world nations to build a global knowledge society for comprehensive peace, prosperity and human development. In this direction, it has already initiated a concerted plan for establishing a better world in this new century. Following certain recommendations of the UN the Republic of Korea, Malaysia and Morocco, have halved the proportion of their people living in poverty.[39] Similarly, the Indian states of Haryana, Kerala and Punjab have achieved in bringing down poverty. Other countries can learn much from their experience and adopt effectively the UN direction noted below.[40]

- Halve, between 1990 and 2015, the proportion of people whose income is less than one dollar a day;
- Halve, between 1990 and 2015, the proportion of people who suffer from hunger and achieve universal primary education;
- Ensure that by 2015 children everywhere — boys and girls alike — will be able to complete a full course of primary schooling and promote gender equality and empower women;
- Eliminate gender disparity in primary and secondary education, preferably by 2005, and at all levels of education not later than 2015 and reduce child mortality;
- Reduce by two-thirds, between 1990 and 2015, the under-five mortality rate and improve maternal health;
- Reduce by three quarters, between 1990 and 2015, the maternal mortality ratio and combat HIV/AIDS, malaria and other diseases;
- Have halted by 2015 and begun to reverse the spread of HIV/AIDS and ensure environmental sustainability;
- Have halted by 2015 and begun to reverse the incidence of malaria and other major diseases and develop a global partnership for development;
- Integrate the principles of sustainable development into country policies and programmes, and reverse the loss of environmental resources;

- Halve by 2015 the proportion of people without sustainable access to safe drinking water;
- To have achieved by 2020 a significant improvement in the lives of at least 100 million slum dwellers;
- Develop a global partnership for development and develop an open, rule-based, non-discriminatory trading and financial system;
- Address the special needs of the least developed countries;
- Address the special needs of landlocked and small island developing States;
- Deal comprehensively with the debt problems of developing countries;
- Develop and implement strategies for decent and productive work for youth in developing countries;
- Provide access, in cooperation with pharmaceutical companies, to affordable essential drugs in developing countries; and
- Make available, in cooperation with the private sector, the benefits of new technologies, especially information and communication technologies.

NOTES

1. See Dan Smith, *The State of War and Peace Atlas* (London: Penguin Publication, 1997), pp. 12–161.
2. *Ibid.*
3. For more details see K. Prabha, *Terrorism : An Instrument of Foreign Policy* (New Delhi : South Asian Publishers, 2000), pp. 13–43.
4. *Ibid.*
5. See the United States (US) *Bureau of the Census, International Data Base* (Washington : The Bureau Press, 2000).
6. *Ibid.*
7. The essays of Thomas Robert Malthus (1766–1834) on the *Principle of Population* remains as one of the important studies even in this century.
8. See the web site http://*www.poverty com*
9. *Ibid.*

10. Cited in Swami Ranganathananda, "Social Responsibilities of Public Administrators", *Peace March* (Dharwad) Vol. 2, No. 9 & 10, October 1999, p.13.
11. See Jean Dreze, 'Starving the Poor', *The Hindu*, (Madras) 18 March, 2001, p. 12
12. See *The Hindu*, 21 March, 2001 and see http://*www.dallasnews.com*
13. *Ibid.*
14. *The Hindu*, 28 March, 2001.
15. See http://*www.aleanation.com*
16. *Ibid.*
17. See http://*www.dallasnews.com,* for more See Caroline Thomas. *Global Governance,* Development and Security (Delhi: Pluto Press, 2001).
18. *Ibid.*
19. See the website *http://www.health.com*
20. See the website *http//www.ncpa.org/pi/internet/index.html*
21. *Ibid.*
22. *The Hindu*, 14 March, 2001.
23. See Kancha Illaiah, 'The Buddha Smiles in Afghanistan', *The Hindu*, 13 March, 2001.
24. See the website n.16
25. *Ibid.*
26. Cited in Mahadev Horatti, "Peace Message for New Millennium", *Peace March*, Vol. 2, No. 9 & 10, Sept.– Oct. 1999, p. 3
27. See Richard Field House and William Arkin, *The Nuclear Battle Fields: Global Links in the Arms Race* (Cambridge: Ballinger, 1985).
28. *Ibid.*
29. *Ibid.*
30. See for more detail on TMD, Keith Payne, *Laser Weapons in Space Policy and Doctrine* (Boulder: Westveiw Press, 1983).
31. *Ibid.*
32. For ABM and Outer Space Treaty, See Josef Gold Blat, *Arms Control Agreements* (New York : Praeger, 1982).
33. See the website, n. 13
34. For a detailed study in this subject, see Noam Chomsky, *Rouge States* (Mumbai: Indian Word Research Press. 2001).
35. See Gilbert Etienne, 'Economy of Leakage and Seepage in Asia', *The Hindu,* 3 March 2001.
36. See Kancha Illaiah, *'The Buddha Smiles'* n. 19

37. For analytical study on this subject, see Theodore A. Columbus and James H. Wolfe, *Introduction to International Relations : Power and Justice* (Prentice Hall of India, 1981).
38. See T.M. Farhathulla, 'A Degeneration in Quality', *The Hindu*, 13 March, 2001.
39. See *The Hindu*, 17 March, 2001.
40. See Swami Ranganathananda, *Social Responsibilities of Public Administrators*, n. 6, p. 13.

Chapter - 2

Nuclear Issues and South Asia

Background

Since the dawn of nuclear age on 2 December 1942 when Enrico Fermi made a chain reaction in a pile of uranium in the University of Chicago, the world nations have been utilizing nuclear energy for both destructive and constructive purposes. In fact, the history of nuclear energy began with the history of nuclear weapon test on 16 July 1945 when the United States exploded the first nuclear bomb, code named 'Trinity' at Alamogordo, New Mexico. The Former Soviet Union was the next country to explode a bomb on 29 August 1949. After the Soviet test, other countries followed in the field were Britain on 3 October 1952; France on 3 December 1960; China on 16 October 1964. In continuation of its exploration into the field of nuclear energy, the US had exploded another thermonuclear bomb—code named 'Mike'— at Eniwetok Atoll in the Pacific on 1 November 1952, which was 500 times more powerful than the Trinity test.[1] Similar tests were also conducted by the former Soviet Union on 22 November 1955, the UK on 8 March 1957; China on 17 June 1967 and by France on 24 August 1968. Thus, more than 2000 tests were conducted world wide—the US with more than 1000, Russia more than 700, France more than 200, the UK more than 40 and China more than 40.

Nuclear tests are carried out in all environments : above ground, under ground and under water. They have occurred on top of towers, onboard barges, from balloons, on the earth's surface, in the depth of 20,000 feet under the sea, in the depth of more than 8,000 feet under the earth, and in horizontal tunnels. The tests sites are located all over the world. In Pacific—Bikini Atoll (US); Christmas Island (US/UK); Eniwetok Atoll (US); Fangataufa Atoll (France); Johnston Atoll (US); Malden Island (UK); Mororua Atoll (France); Monte Bello Island in Australia; Emu Fields (UK); Maralinga (UK). There are many sites within the US, which include Nevada, Alamogordo, Hattiesburg, Grand Valley, Colorado, Rifle, Farmington, Hot Creek Valley, Central Nevada, Fallon, and Amchitka.

The former Soviet test sites include Novaya Zemlya, Semipalatinsk in eastern Kazakhstan; Azgir and Astrakhan in western Kazakhstan; near Oren burg between the Volga River and the Ural mountains in the Ukraine, Uzbekistan and in Turkmenistan. The French test sites include Reggane in Algeria and Hoggar Massif at In Ecker. China has Lop Nor test site in Xingjian Province. In India the tests are carried out at Pokhran in Rajasthan and Pakistan in Chagai Hill. It was reported that due to underground tests, approximately 3900 kg of plutonium has been left in the ground and due to atmospheric tests 4,200 kg of plutonium has been discharged into the atmosphere of the world.[2]

In the case of exploring the nuclear energy for constructive purposes, it was only after the successful establishment of a nuclear power plant by the United Kingdom on 21 February 1956, many nations had shown interest for utilizing the nuclear energy for electricity purposes. Nuclear power plants need less fuel than the one needed for burning fossil fuels. For example, one ton of uranium produces more energy than the one produced by several million tons of coal or several million barrels of oil. Moreover, coal and oil burning plants pollute the air, whereas a well-maintained nuclear power plant does not release contaminants into the environment.

Nuclear energy is used for digging channel, preserving food, removing mountain, producing electricity, X-ray and for constructing nuclear bombs. United States, Russia, the United Kingdom, France, China are the leading powers in both the fields. Today, there are 435 nuclear power plants operating all over the world generating about 3,45,000 MW of electricity in 32 countries, about one-sixth of the world's electricity supply. For instance, France generates 76 per cent of its electricity from nuclear power plants; Belgium — 56 per cent, South Korea—36 per cent, Switzerland—40 per cent, Sweden—47 per cent, Finland—30 per cent, Japan—33 per cent and the United Kingdom—25 per cent, Bulgaria—46 per cent, Hungary—42 per cent, and the Czech Republic and Slovakia combined-20 per cent. Although the US is not the leader in percentage, it has the largest total electric output from nuclear power: 98,000 MWe from 105 plants, generating around 20 per cent of its electric power.[3]

Understanding the Nuclear Energy

Nuclear reaction is a natural one. All materials, as scientifically known, contain component of elements that bind them as different energy-entities. Depending upon the number of components, for example, protons, electrons and neutrons, they differ in structure and capacity of giving out energy.[4] The best scientific example is the reaction phenomenon that takes place in the sun and the stars. They are seemingly inexhaustible sources of energy due to nuclear reactions in which matter is converted into energy. The scientists of the world community had exploited these natural mechanisms and put them in use for generating massive nuclear power through artificial reactors. Reactors are nothing but a fuel-containing cylinder like machines that withstand all the heat prodnced by the nuclear reaction within.[5] As a result today the world energy, for instance in the production of electricity constitute more than twenty per cent of the nuclear energy.

Technical Process

For producing nuclear energy, two different methods—fission and fusion are adopted. In fission a large nuclei are split to release energy and in fusion method, small nuclei are combined to release energy. It is paramount to understand each of them technically. In nuclear fission, the nuclei of atoms are split through which the atomic bomb and nuclear reactors work. Uranium is the main fuel used to undergo nuclear fission, as shooting neutrons at them can easily split its nuclei. In addition, once a uranium nucleus is split multiple neutrons are released which split other uranium nuclei. This phenomenon is known as a chain reaction.[6] It has to be noted that the Atomic bombs produced by US in this process were dropped in the cities of Hiroshima and Nagasaki on 6 and 9 August 1945 killing over 1,40,000 people together. It is not that only the fission reactors are used for electricity purposes alone. They are also being used for powering the ships and spacecrafts. For example, the US uses the fission reactors—usually the pressurized water reactors with energy conversion based on steam-turbine cycle, for powering its ships extensively. It has built totally155 missile submarines, nine guided missile cruisers (18 reactors), and five aircraft carriers with 24 reactors and has operated 9 prototype reactors on land. Of this total, 22 submarines are decommissioned or non-operational. Fission reactors are also used in commercial ships. For instance, the Russians use it in Icebreaker, *Lenin* and the US in the *NS Savannah*.[7]

In nuclear fusion, as stated above, the nuclei of atoms are combined or fused together similar to the energy-producing process takes place in the sun and stars. In the core of the sun at temperatures of 10–15 million degrees Celsius, hydrogen is converted into helium providing enough energy to sustain life on earth.[8] For energy production on earth, different fusion reactions are involved. The most suitable reaction occurs between the nuclei of the two heavy isotopes of hydrogen—deuterium and tritium. Through fusion method hydrogen bombs, known as thermonuclear bomb, are produced. Hydrogen bombs are thousands of time more powerful than the atomic bomb.[9] Such bomb was successfully testified first by the American scientists on 1 November 1952.

Usually, such innovative efforts in understanding and developing new nuclear science based on new material by the

US were initiated with the interests of attaining technical superiority and military advantage. With this objective, the Department of Defence (DOD) plans to develop military capabilities with the help of superior technology. The Americans confer two important reasons for initiating a new material programme in the nuclear field. The first is to overcome a projected threat and the second is to incorporate new technology. Overcoming a projected threat is a battlefield imperative, if not achieved the adversary's capabilities in the field would jeopardize the ability of the US to fight and win the war.

The second reason, according to them, is that incorporating newer technology into an existing one increases the operational capability, enhances system reliability or reduces costs of the US that takes care of competing with enemy in the nuclear field by exploring into a new avenue. Such activities, as they argue, not only help develop the field alone but also reduce the logistics burden.[10] It should be noted here that the process of incorporating new technology into existing or future systems is commonly referred as research and development (R&D).

The Case of South Asia

In South Asia, only India and Pakistan have been involving into nuclear activities for both constructive and destructive purposes. India established its Atomic Energy Commission in 1948 and built a research reactor, *Apsara,* with thermal output of 8,000 KW. east of Mumbai under the direction of Dr. Homi J. Bhabha. *Apsara* was the first nuclear reactor in Asia.[11] It has to be noted here that China was not a communist country by that time. India's quest for nuclear energy was demonstrated by passing yet another milestone as Plutonium production reactor, Cirius, was built at Bhabha Atomic Research Centre *(BARC)* in 1960. Followed by this, *Dhruva* reactor was made operative in 1985. Further, with its rich experience it went ahead constructing reprocessing plants at Trombay, Tarapur in 1980's, and at Kalpakkam in 1999. A nuclear plant is being under construction at present at Koodamkulam in Tamil Nadu with the help of Russia. However, India's ambition for nuclear energy was criticized by many countries when India succeeded its first underground nuclear test in 1974.

Although the Government of India announced that the test was conducted for peaceful purpose, the scientist Raja Ramana who was heading the project confessed that it was a bomb.[12] Thus India had been undeclared nuclear power since 1974, the year when the test was carried in Pokharan desert in Rajasthan. In the same place, it has demonstrated series of nuclear tests on 11 and 13 May 1998 and declared itself that it had become the sixth nuclear power in the world. India claimed that it had involved in five well-planned tests that yielded expected results. According to India, it tested a low yield device (0.2 KT), a fission device (12 KT), a fusion device (43 KT), and 2 devices with the yield of below 1 KT (0.3–0.5 KT).[13]

The American observers disputed the claim of India. According to them, India had demonstrated high-level nuclear technology but not the one needed for thermonuclear bomb. Nevertheless, Government of India reported that tests of hydrogen bomb with the yield of 45 KT and a fission bomb with the yield of 15 KT were successful and, therefore, it could have thermonuclear technology. As a counter measure, Pakistan had tested its first bomb at Chagai Hills nearer to the border of Afghanistan on 28 May 1998. Followed by the tests it declared emergency throughout the country on 29 May and went for fulfilling its ambition by testing yet another test on 30 May.[14]

National Interest of India

India's intention to become nuclear weapons power is based on its interest of national security for which, as stated, it would need to develop effective and reliable deterrent by means of minimum nuclear forces.[15] Its military doctrine, therefore, must aim at demonstrating its substantial military ability to China and Pakistan. For such deterrent posture, India justifies of using nuclear energy for developing weapons. According to the Indian National Defence Report (INDR) 1998–1999, it would develop such deterrent only against the countries threatening to use weapons of mass destruction and it would never use its nuclear weapons first against any countries in the world. The National Security Advisory Board (NSAB) of India has also noted on 17 August 1999 that Indian nuclear doctrine was aimed at pursuing, as noted above, an effective and reliable deterrent.[16]

However, it is not clear as to how many weapons it would need in the future and how many of them it has already produced. The Washington based National Resources Defense Council (NRDC) states that India has about fifty bombs with the yield of ten to fifteen kiloton.[17] India, nonetheless, has the capacity for acquisition of fissile material and for designing and manufacturing weapons by itself. Its fissile material and natural resources are enough to meet out its demand in the future. Since it has got enough reprocessing technology related facilities, the Pu-239 production facilities and tritium production facilities needed for sophisticated nuclear weapons, it can go ahead in the pursuit of fusion technology. According to reports, India has been trying on improving of safety, reliability and size suitable for a missile.[18] At present, it is considering the plan for carrying out a non-critical test and a computer simulation test, launch of a test missile, development of a smaller warhead, a longer-range missile, and a safer and more precise reentry technique.

The former President A.P.J. Abdul Kalam, a scientist who earned the epithet of 'missile man' has defended India's interest for missile production pointing out that it had declared 'no first use policy' and, therefore, it could keep the option for producing missile. More importantly India's interest in this field should be seen in the light of its natural resources especially thorium, which is massively available in India.[19] It is noted that more than seventy-five per cent of the thorium of the world is located in India. Thorium can be utilized for production of energy through nuclear means, which would obviously be used like in any other countries of the world either for deterrent or for production of energy that will place India economically powerful nation of the world in the twenty first century.[20]

Nuclear Interest of Pakistan

Pakistan had constructed its first nuclear reactor PARR-T in Islamabad in 1965 and its second one, PARR-U in Karachi in 1970, which are covered by the safeguard agreement singed with the International Atomic Energy Agency (IAEA). The former Prime Minister of Pakistan, Zulfikar Ali Bhutto had decided to develop nuclear weapon in 1972. It should be noted that India's victory over Pakistan in three wars were seriously being viewed by the leaders of Pakistan which influenced the decision of the then Prime Minister Bhutto to manufacture bomb even if the people of Pakistan were forced to eat grass because of economic poverty in the process of spending state's money on bomb.[21] Initially France did not help Pakistan. However, it helped later on for its own strategic reason.

Nevertheless, Pakistan could generate its support from China especially for constructing a reprocessing facility at Chashma near the Indus River. The enrichment facility at Kahuta was constructed under the direction of Dr. Abdul Qadeer Khan who came back from Europe in 1976. In 1980, it had involved in developing a Hiroshima-type atomic weapon made of U-235.[22] Throughout 1980s, Pakistan was very active in pursuing its nuclear ambition. In 1984, it was reported that Pakistan had possibly manufactured a uranium type atomic bomb and tested it. Continuing its pursuit, plutonium production reactor PARR-V was built at Khushab in 1995.

Pakistan tested Ghauri missile in 1998 and in the same year, as counter measure to India's nuclear tests, it also tested nuclear devices on 28 and 30 May. Although Prime Minister Nawaz Sharif and Foreign Minister Gohar Ayub Khan spoke about the tests, it is worth noting the statement of Dr. A.Q. Khan, the father of Pakistani nuclear bomb, who stated, "one of five devices yielded 30-35 KT, about twice the yield of the Hiroshima bomb. The other four devices were low yield warheads for a tactical missile. We have used an advanced enrichment technology. A uranium type device is seldom used in the world, but the efficiency and the reliability are very high. At least one hole is left for a further test. We will not test in the near future."[23] Many countries disputed this view. For example, according to US, the largest yield was 10 KT, and the rest of it is eight kiloton in total.

However, it is clear that Pakistan has demonstrated its capacity for producing a number of small size nuclear weapons and its possession of free-fall atomic bombs and boosted bombs made of U-235.[24] It has sufficient technology and facilities for acquiring weapon-grade enriched uranium (WEU). It is reported that Pakistan has the capability to produce 110 kg of WEU kg per year. Its capability for acquiring Plutonium through Khushab reactor is estimated to be 10–15 kg per year. According to one report Pakistani production capability of WEU is estimated about 5–10 bombs per year. It has mastered, as reported, in the fields of design and manufacturing uranium type atomic bomb and a boosted bomb. It has been now developing a thermonuclear weapon and a Pu type atomic bomb by improving the reliability. Pakistan's missile programme include IRBM Ghauri, AIRBM Ghauri, BSRBM Shaheen and CSRBM Shaheen.[25] Many more missiles are also being made.

Pakistan's intention to become a nuclear power is to counter act against India. It considers India as a number one antagonistic power. Its pro-deterrent argument lies on the premises that India is superior in both conventional and nuclear deterrent and, therefore, it has to prepare nuclear deterrent as counter force. As a result, Pakistan has rejected India's offer of a No-first-use treaty of a nuclear weapon. Instead, it demanded India to sign up either an Anti war pact or Non-aggression pact. Although National Command Headquarters (NCH) was established on 3 February 2000 for looking after Pakistan's nuclear policy, nuclear force management and developments, its nuclear policy is not clearly codified yet.[26] China, North Korea, Saudi Arabia and United Arab Emirates are fervent supporters of Pakistani nuclear ambition apart from the technical, moral and political supports of the US.

Critical Lessons

Nuclear explosion generates radiation, which is harmful to the cells of human body. It makes people sick and in course of time it kills them. A person exposed to nuclear radiation undergoes a long-term suffering. In addition, it affects the person even after twenty years without showing any symptom in the initial period of his exposure to radiation. People get exposed to such radiation due to reactor disaster, known as a meltdown. In such an accident, the fission reaction goes out of control, leading to a nuclear explosion and the emission of great amount of radiation.[27] In 1979, due to the failure of the cooling system of a nuclear reactor at the Three Mile Island near Harrisburg, Pennsylvania in the US, radiation leaked causing a great deal of human suffering.

In 1986, a worst disaster struck Russia's Chernobyl nuclear power plant to which several dozen died and thousands of people exposed to radiation are reportedly suffering from cancer even today. Yet another problem the reactors create in the process of making nuclear energy is the disposal of waste material.[28] Such material emits dangerous radiation that could kill people who touch them. They are stored in special cooling pools at the nuclear reactors themselves and managed properly. The United States plans to move its nuclear waste to a remote underground dump by the year 2010. The dumped nuclear waste material can explode like bombs due to pressure inside the earth. Such incident took place in the former Soviet Union in 1957 at a dump site of Ural Mountains killing many people.[29]

Recent Developments

The US has been involving scientists to produce hydrogen based nuclear energy science 2003. According to US plan, popularly known as the Bush-Cheney energy plan, productions of nuclear power reactors are also possible based on hydrogen-2. Generally, H_2 does not exist by itself naturally. It can be separated from water through various ways such as thermo chemical, electrolysis and steam electrolysis. Bacteria and algae can also produce H_2 as a waste product. Current hydrogen separation processes use fossil fuels to raise the temperature enough to separate H_2 from either water or natural gas. This process releases greenhouse gases whether or not one is separating water or natural gas. However, additional carbon dioxide is also released into the air as a by-product of natural gas separation. Separation of water results only in oxygen as by-product. Since CO_2 is one of the gases responsible for climate destruction, use of fossil fuels in these separation processes is not environmentally friendly.[30] Therefore, while cars running on H_2 fuel would give us clean air in one respect, producing the hydrogen would still contribute to climate decimation.

As of the reasons, many in the US oppose the energy plan of the former President Bush, which is according to them, a new generation of nuclear energy not anything else. The Government of US encourages this sort of plan because it runs out of uranium and digging uranium out of the ground is more expensive. As a result, the US is concentrating in the H_2 production technology using nuclear means. According to the Phoenix Project, 12 million one-megawatt wind energy systems could provide the entire energy required for the country including the power needed for 17 million cars manufactured every year in the country.[31]

A New Nuclear Order—Proliferation Security Initiative (PSI)

It is necessary to look at the historical routs for managing nuclear energy crisis before understanding the new initiative. In the beginning of the 1950s, many countries were active in proposing to curtail the spread of nuclear energy especially with reference to the usage of this energy for production of weapons. To this effect, in 1958, Ireland, proposed specific resolutions to the United Nations General Assembly (UNGA) aimed at preventing the misuse of nuclear energy. Followed by this proposal, in 1961, Sweden introduced a new resolution with the plan of defining the nuclear weapon countries as well as countries striving genuinely for energy. It was objected by Netherlands as it was playing an important role in NATO.

Sweden's initiative, however, was supported by the former Soviet Union, which was objecting to NATO for stationing nuclear weapons in Europe, particularly in Germany. It should be noted here that according to NATO, it was stationing nuclear weapons in Europe to balance the overwhelming conventional superiority of the former Soviet Union and the Warsaw Pact. As a result, the non-proliferation issues had become the dominant agenda item at the Eighteen Nations Disarmament Committee (ENDC) in 1965.[32] In 1966, when negotiations came to an end the non-aligned countries appealed to the big countries for curtailing the nuclear tests itself. Nevertheless, in the end of the discussion the then US President Johnson initiated bilateral negotiations with the former Soviet Union, which contributed to the formation of the NPT in full form later on.

During that period, India took the position that a good non-proliferation treaty should contain a prohibition on the production of nuclear weapons for all states, including the nuclear weapon states and that the treaty should contain a binding agreement on nuclear disarmament. Other countries did not agree with the Indian position. Canada, for example, argued for practical measure on guarantee in line with the US. India approach has, however, brought in certain good measure. In the draft of January 18 1968, an article was included in which the nuclear weapon states promised to negotiate in good faith on effective measures relating to the cessation of the nuclear arms race at an early date.[33] Subsequently the NPT was opened for signature on July 1 1968. In the review conferences of 1975,

1985, 1990 and 1995 the signatories of the treaty failed to reach agreement on a final text due to disagreements related to nuclear disarmament, and in particular to a comprehensive treaty to ban nuclear testing. Despite, it was decided that the treaty has to be given with the right of continuing in force indefinitely after its extension conferences, as stipulated under Article X of the NPT. [34]

To stress the importance of the unilateral measures regarding tactical nuclear weapons that President Bush announced within a month after the Moscow coup of August 1991 that all nuclear artillery and all short-range missiles on land and all tactical weapons deployed in ships and submarines must be withdrawn. President Gorbachev too reciprocated with a comparable package. Some time later, just after the dissolution of the Soviet Union, President Bush announced an important unilateral measures with regard to the reduction of strategic nuclear weapons, including halting the development of the Midget man ICBM. In connection with his initiative START II was signed in January 1993, which aimed at reducing the number of strategic nuclear weapons to 3,000 and 3,500 respectively.[35]

Followed by Bush, President Clinton declared that the US would try to achieve a Comprehensive Test Ban Treaty (CTBT) with the support from many countries in the Conference on Disarmament in Geneva. His initiative, although many countries in the beginning supported it, was resulted in a multilateral cutoff treaty, an agreement to end production of all fissile materials for nuclear weapons purposes in the CD meet of 1996. Although the number of party to CTBT has increased slowly over the years and now exceeding 170, it could not be implemented yet due to the indifferent attitude of the US. Nuclear Non-proliferation Treaty (NPT) was hailed once by the US. Now it is denounced by it. In addition, it proposed in 2003 for a new Proliferation Security Initiative (PSI).

The PSI calls for prohibition of international traffic in sensitive nuclear materials through cooperative actions by the naval and air forces of friendly nations. In support of PSI,

President George Bush has proposed in February 2004 a seven-point nuclear agenda that highlights the inadequacy of the present regime—NPT and supports the principle of effective non-proliferation. His agenda aims at drawing in law enforcement agencies to crack down on networks of nuclear smuggling of the type developed by Dr. A.Q. Khan in Pakistan.[36] It should be noted that India, being the victim of clandestine nuclear activities between Pakistan and North Korea, may be interested in the new initiative especially in preventing the international trafficking of sensitive materials.

A.Q Khan's Syndrome and the Aftermath

A.Q. Khan has earned the epithets of 'bomb man of Pakistan' and the father of 'Islamic bomb'. With his solid experience that he had acquired from his long association with many European as well as North American countries during 1970s and 1980s, he has been involving into nuclear activities of other countries in the world, which has become an unprecedented one in the history of nuclear proliferation. The Americans' blame against him of having assisted nuclear weapon programme of North Korea, the country that had given up its nuclear pursuit in 1994 through an agreement signed with the US, has now become very important in the light of the development of controlling nuclear proliferation in the globalizing world of today.

Western intelligence experts alleged that A.Q. Khan's Research Laboratory (KRL) near Rawalpindi provided the design for a uranium centrifuge to North Korea in exchange for help in developing the medium range Ghauri missile, which is identical to North Korea's Nodong missile.[37] Although the fact that Abdul Qadeer Khan had been in the network of having accessibility with nuclear establishments and potential nuclear scientists throughout his career, his activities are now being seriously considered especially in connection with the PSI plan of the US. It is important to note that the uranium enrichment plant at Kahuta, where the bomb material is made, was built on the basis of technical information stolen from Holland where in A.Q. Khan was working during 1970s.

Between 1970s and 1980s, Pakistani agencies functioning in the Western Europe and North America were procuring various equipment and material required for the Kahuta plant in clandestine manner. High frequency power generators, high-speed flash camera, systems for making uranium hexafluoride, special purpose valves and some of the steel based raw items were smuggled by these agencies.[38] Although, they were charged with complaints by the Western Governments, the Pakistan Government was not very keen in dealing with them rather it was encouraging such unlawful activities.

By such illegal activities, Pakistan had built Kahuta plant to produce nuclear weapon material for which the European and North American countries, especially Holland, were also responsible. In the later stages of its quest for nuclear weapons, Pakistan received from China the design as well as the trigger devices for nuclear weapon. As of now, Pakistan is equipped with a number of nuclear weapons. It is worth noting here that a distinguished American foreign policy analyst, Selig Harrison, in his article published in *International Herald* tribune, states that Pakistan has now 48 nuclear weapons and enough fissile material in storage to make 52 more, thus making a total of 100.

Having such an impressive smuggling experience, the Pakistani agencies are covertly assisting many countries in the nuclear field in which A.Q. Khan, being the leader, plays a dominant role. John Wolfsthal, a former weapons adviser to US Energy Department, stated once that A.Q Khan had visited uranium rich nation and helped many countries in their effort for making nuclear weapons. According to him he visited uranium rich countries like Sudan, Mali Nigeria and Niger, which are suspected to have uranium deposit and helped Libya, North Korea and Iran in their nuclear weapon programme. More importantly, as he noted that he had visited North Korea alone over a dozen times before 2001.[39] It is also alleged that Pakistan had received funds over the period for its nuclear activities from Saudi Arabia and in turn, it helped many senior Saudi Ministers to have access to the sensitive Pakistani facilities.

However, Pakistani association with Saudi Arabia is not very revealing, as no one knows about the secrecy behind their strategic links. It is believed by many western experts that it may help the terrorists as there are number Saudi scientists and politicians have contact with Al- Qaeda and Osama Bin Laden. In this connection, a report states that a top Al-Qaeda operative, Khalid Sheikh Mohammed, had a clandestine meeting with A.Q. Khan in the early 2003. However, Mohammed denied it later on when he was arrested in the same year. Although the US imposed sanctions on KRL and Changgwang Sinyong Corporation of North Korea for nuclear proliferation activities and President Musharraf removed Dr. A.Q. Khan from his responsibility by enacting law that bans the Pakistani scientist meeting with the North Korean counterparts, incidents with regard to unlawful activities in the field is not scaled down completely, which is needed for securing the non proliferation regime.[40]

Conclusion

Since India and Pakistan have become nuclear weapon powers and more than seventy five per cent of the world thorium resource, as noted above, is located in India, the region has strategic advantage in the future of world economy. Therefore, managing energy as well as political crisis between nations in the region is very important to be dealt with. Nuclear energy, though being used in this region for weapon purposes, comparatively it is not posing greater danger as India and Pakistan have declared their interests for minimum deterrent. In the constructive side of the energy, both of them are not too ambitious, as they have no such plans for producing huge energy based on nuclear sources.

The dream in the nuclear field, however, has to be realized

in the light of the development of globalization process that influences the security and economic environment of the world community. Nonetheless, they should play very responsible role to protect not only their interests but also the interests of all other countries in this region. Thus, the management of nuclear energy, both destructive and constructive, lies in the hands of world community, which would possibly establish in this decade of the new millennium a 'new order for nuclear energy security' in a comprehensive way encompassing issues relating to all the regions of the world including South Asia.

NOTES

1. See Frank G. Dawson, *Nuclear Power Development and Management of a Technology* (Seattle: University of Washington Press, 1976), pp. 162–170
2. See *http://www.i-b-r.org/*
3. *Ibid.*
4. See Frank G. Dawson, *Nuclear Power Development and Management of Technology*, No.1, pp. 68–70
5. *Ibid.*
6. See Harvey W. Graves Jr., *Nuclear Fuel Management* (New York: John Wiley Press, 1979), pp. 28–33
7. *Ibid.*, the fissionable material are plutonium-239, uranium-233, and thorium–232
8. *Ibid.*
9. Deuterium is abundant as it is available in all forms of water. Its supply would last for millions of years. Tritium does not occur naturally. It is manufactured from Lithium, the light metal, which is plentiful in the earth's crust. It will last for at least 1000 years. Ten grams of deuterium, which can be extracted from 500 litres of water and 15 g of tritium produced from 30 g of extracted of lithium, would produce enough fuel for the lifetime electricity needs of an average person. See *Nuclear Fuel Management*, No. 6, pp. 8–10
10. In this process, the Americans introduced new technology transfer methods, dual use technology, accelerated transition, horizontal technology integration, technology insertion, modelling and simulation and advanced technology demonstration. They also

introduced methods of displaying information with regard to advanced concepts and technology programme, concept experimentation programme, advanced war fighting experiment, technology demonstrations, small business innovation research programme, fast track programme, limited objective experiments, product improvement programmes, funding categories for research and development programmes and strategic research objectives war fighting capability. *Ibid.* pp. 9-10

11. See Birla Institute of Scientific Research, *India and the Atom* (New Delhi: Allied Publishers, 1982), pp. 60–70
12. *Ibid.*
13. *Ibid.*
14. *The Hindu* (Chennai) 31 May 1998.
15. *Ibid.*
16. *The Hindu,* 18 August, 1999.
17. http://www.i-b-r.org/
18. *Ibid.*
19. *Ibid.*
20. *Ibid.*
21. For detailed study on Pakistan nuclear programme, see Sinha and Subramanian, *Nuclear Pakistan* (New Delhi: Vision Books, 1980), pp. 49–56
22. *Ibid.*
23. *The Hindu,* 31 May, 1998.
24. See P.K. Ghosh, "India Pakistan Nuclear Parity: Is it Feasible or Necessary", Na.21, pp. 522–524.
25. *Ibid.*
26. *The Hindu,* 4 February, 2000.
27. See Harvey W. Graves Jr., *Nuclear Fuel Management,* No.6, pp. 30-32
28. *Ibid.*
29. *Ibid.*
30. See Vol://www.i-b-r.org/
31. *Ibid.*
32. See Frank G. Dawson, Nuclear Power Development and Management of a Technology, No. 1, pp. 162–170
33. *Ibid.*
34. *Ibid.*
35. *Ibid.*

36. See *New Indian Express* (Chennai), 19 February, 2004.
37. *Nucleonic Week,* November 6, cited in *Strategic Digest*, New Delhi). Vol. 33, No. 12, December 2003, p.1456.
38. *Ibid.*
39. *Strategic Digest,* Vol. 33, No. 6 June 2003, pp. 488–489.
40. *Ibid.*

Chapter - 3

Combating Terrorism in South Asia

Introduction

Terrorism has been a threat to civil society since time immemorial. However, an organized form of human violence was recorded in 1214 in the history of international relation.[1] Since there is no a standard definition for the concept of terrorism, it is imperative to view that all forms of violence against organized life of human beings are terrorism. Motives of terrorism, therefore, do not matter whatsoever they are. Although the number of human violence has been waning at present unlike during the period of the 19th century to the mid of the 20th century, its manifestation in the style of functioning has been intensified and convoluted by the means of using sophisticated high-tech weapons Inspite of the fact that the world community continues counter terrorist acts, the terrorists' organizations are persistently promoting it in many regions.

Prominent among such organizations include primarily the Islamic extremist groups Hamas, the Palestinian Islamic Jihad, Hizballah, Al-Faida and Al-Qaeda. These organizations have connections with different terrorist networks in the world. Kashmir is one of the worst affected regions in this respect.[2] The global attention on international terrorism was, in fact, drawn when the terrorist initiated attack on World Trade Centre (WTC) of the US in 1993 by the suicide bombers that led to the recent attack in the same place by September 11, 2001 killing more than six thousand people hailing from eighty nations. Unequivocally denouncing of these acts of terrorists, the United

Nations Security Council (UNSC) unanimously adopted a comprehensive anti-terrorism resolution in 1973, which put forward strategy for combating terrorism in the world.[3] Against this background, this chapter deals with terrorism in South Asia especially referring to the problems of India in the recent times.

Concept and History

The concept of terrorism, as noted above, is not well defined yet. Every nation defines it according to its own interest and political convenience. However, it is generally being agreed that terrorism is the calculated use of violence or the threat of violence to inculcate fear; intended to coerce or to intimidate governments or societies in the pursuit of goals that are generally political, religious, or ideological.[4] Thus, it includes all kinds of organized human violence in its definition. In the earlier years, terrorists avoided attacks on innocent people and excluded women, children and the elderly people. They were very careful in selecting their targets. For example, in late 19th century extremists in the Former Soviet Union who planned to kill Tsar Alexander-II avoided their effort thinking that the attack might hurt innocent people.

Nevertheless, in the early twentieth century, terrorists began to attack the people and started changing their tactics especially by selecting the most vulnerable targets with the sole aim of generating political pressure. At present the terrorist actions include the traditional assassinations, bombings, arson, hostage taking, hijacking, kidnapping, seizure and occupation of a building, attacks on a facility, sabotage, and perpetration of hoaxes. Their operative methods include new categories high-tech weapons including nuclear, biological, and chemical.[5]

Similarly, the related concepts such as antiterrorism and counter terrorism are also agreed upon a common understanding of the definition. According to the definition, it concerns about the defensive measures against terrorists while the counter terrorism about the offensive measures. The counter measures aim at preventing, deterring and responding the terrorist acts.[6]

Whereas the antiterrorism aims at preventing attacks and minimizing the effects of the attack, weakening the terrorist organizations and their political power and making the potential targets more difficult to be attacked by the terrorists. Anti-terrorism, also include the physical and operational security of the personnel involved in counter terrorist activities. The overall understanding of the terrorism through this definition, therefore, lies on the logic that combating terrorism is the individual right of self-defence, which is universally recognized in the legal system of the entire world. The only problem is that one should differentiate between those perpetrating, aiding, or abetting terrorism and others who might sympathize with their cause but do not engage in violent acts.[7]

Nonetheless, terrorism for various reasons have been organized and let loose on innocent people in the world from the very beginning. It reached its peak when the terrorists have started using human beings as careers of explosives. It should be noted that the suicide bomb culture by the terrorists were set off by the Hizballah, which had claimed responsibility for bombing of the Israeli Embassy in 1992. Followed by this, Jewish cultural center in Buenos Aires in 1994, and Panamanian commuter aircraft in the same year were attacked by the terrorists. Israeli Consulate and a building housing Jewish organization in London were also attacked in the subsequent years. Terrorist launched their attack again on Palestinians in Hebron in 1994.[8]

The dangerous spots in the world for terrorist atrocity, next to India, are Palestine and Israel. Because of the intensification of the terrorist activities in these nations, both Israel and Palestine have decided to agree the Oslo peace process that promoted assistance to the Palestinians and economic development in Gaza and the West Bank. Despite, the terrorist atrocities in the region are not yet under control. Rather it exceeds spreading into various Islamic nations like Algeria, Egypt, Iraq, Libya, Lebanon Syria, Sudan and Iran. In fact, the Islamic extremists, after capturing power in Sudan and Iran, have been ruling the respective countries without any trouble.[9] These nations are also reported to be giving asylum to various terrorist groups. It was doubted that Osama Bin Laden has good connections in these countries for his holy war.

Saudi Arabia, as a home country of Osama, has helped his movement to grow. Out of 19 terrorists involved in the September 11 attack, it is found that 11 of them were from Saudi Arabia. Many of the terrorists also seek asylum in Libya, Iraq, Algeria and Egypt. It should be noted that an Egyptian terrorist also participated in the September 11 attack. All these countries, despite their affiliation and interests, have been affected by terrorism. In the Latin American region, Cuba was worst affected because of its role in accommodating terrorist outfits. It is the condition in the cases of both North Korea, and Damascus. They are also doubted to be providing asylum and sponsoring terrorism in the world.[10]

The Case of India

India has lost more than seventy thousand people and two Prime Ministers—Mrs. Indira Gandhi and Mr. Rajiv Gandhi— as victims for the terrorist acts. Almost everyday, terrorist attack on innocent people in some parts of the country is being reported. Generally, terrorist activities in India are supported by Pakistan, Bangladesh, China and Myanmar. Pakistan has been encouraging terrorist activities more than any other countries since its partition in 1947 with the sole aim of capturing the entire Jammu and Kashmir.[11] It waged war in October 1947 with India immediately after the independence and captured almost half of the territory of Jammu and Kashmir in January 1948 when the UN intervened and helped end the war. It should be noted that out of 2,22,236 sq km of Jammu and Kashmir, Pakistan occupied 83,294 sq km of which 5,180 sq km was given to China. China, by 1962 war, had occupied 37,555 sq km. Thus, India has lost 1,20,849 sq km of Jammu and Kashmir.[12]

After seeing the embarrassing defeat of India by China in the 1962 war, Pakistan had attacked India by April 1965 in the

Runn of Kutch with the help of the US. Nevertheless, it was overpowered by India. However, Pakistan did not put down its plan for capturing Kashmir as a whole. As of the reason, it organized a special military force, Al Mujahid, in which thousands of people in POK areas were recruited and trained by Chinese. Later on, a separate military force called Al Burq was organized exclusively to involve in subversive activities in India.[13] Pakistan government from the very beginning has been misusing the people of POK for terrorist activities. People living in the region are not taken care either by the local government or by the Pakistan government. They are extremely struggling for running their routine life. Mostly they earn their livelihood by being loyal to the Pakistan agents or by being joined in the Pakistan run terrorist camps. The unemployed youths are, therefore, forced to join the militant groups for their livelihood. Exploiting the economic condition, terrorists' camps are run in different places in POK and in Pakistan. Familiar among such camps are run in Muzzafarabad and Skardu.

However, Pakistan's covert activities were intensified by cultivating various terrorist groups for subversive activities in India only after it lost the liberation war of Bangladesh in 1971. More than twenty terrorist groups have been reportedly developed by Pakistan, which are involved in subversive activities in India. More prominent among all are as follows:[14]

- Jammu & Kashmir Liberation Front (JKLF)
- Jamat-i-Islami
- Jaish-e-Mohammed
- Hizbul Mujahideen
- Students Liberation Front
- Mahaz-e-Azadi
- Islamic Students League
- People's League
- Islamic Jamat-e-Tulba
- The Muslim Janbaz Force

- Ikhwane Muslimeen
- Allah Tigers
- Hizb-ul-Islami
- Harket-al-Jehad/Ansar
- Lakshar-e-Toiba
- Markaz-e-Dawaul Irshad

For example, Lakshar-e-Toiba has been involving into terrorist activities in Kashmir for more than fifty years now. Although the Pakistani government in 1990 banned some of the groups, their members are inducted in different capacity in the existing terrorist groups. Terrorists involved in the December 1999 hijacking of the Indian flight were tactfully released. They obtained 100 million dollars from Government of India for releasing all the passengers including a dead body of the young man who bored the flight after his honeymoon trip to Nepal and who put up some resistance to the terrorists. The released terrorists include Maulana Azhar, founder of Jaish-e-Mohammed, and Sheikh Umar who shared a part of the ransom amount to Mohammed Atta, who was doubted to be the mastermind of the September 11 attacks in US. The details of terrorist incidents in India in 2000 are noted below just to know about the activisms of the terrorist network in South Asia.[15]

- On 27 February, a bomb exploded at a railroad in New Delhi and injured eight persons apart from causing major damage to the railroad. It was suspected that either Kashmiri Militants or Sikhs could have involved in this incident.
- 3 March, a bomb was exploded on a bus in Sirhand, Punjab, killing eight persons and injuring seven others. This incident was also doubted to be the handiwork of the above mentioned groups.
- 21 March armed militants killed 35 Sikhs in Chadisinghpoora Village. Lashkar-e-Taiba and the Hizbul-Mujahedin were suspected in the massacre.

- 27 March a bomb exploded at the main gate of a military base in Srinagar, killing six military personnel and three civilians and injuring 23 civilians. The Jaish-e-Mohammed and Jamiat-ul-Mujahedin claimed responsibility.
- 3 April armed militants threw a grenade at a group of police officers in Srinagar. The bomb missed the target but exploded in a public place killing three civilians and injuring 11 others. The Hizb-ul-Mujahedin was suspected to be responsible.
- 4 April militants using a remote-controlled device detonated a car bomb near an army convoy in Srinagar, killing one bystander, according to press reports. No one claimed responsibility.
- 15 April armed militants killed 12 persons, wounded seven others, and torched several huts in Tripura, according to press reports. No one claimed responsibility.
- 20 April militants using a remote-controlled device detonated a car bomb near an army convoy in Srinagar, killing one bystander, according to press reports. No one claimed responsibility.
- 28 April a bomb exploded at a police checkpoint in Srinagar, killing one civilian and wounding four police officers and one civilian, according to press reports. No one claimed responsibility.
- In Srinagar, militants threw a grenade at a security patrol but hit a bus stop instead, injuring two civilians, according to press accounts. No one claimed responsibility.
- 10 May in Kupwara, armed militants kidnapped a civilian from his residence and then killed him, according to press reports. No one claimed responsibility.
- 11 May in Bihar, according to press reports, armed militants killed 11 persons and injured four others. No one claimed responsibility.
- 15 May a landmine exploded in Chabran, killing

Kashmir's power minister and four other government employees and destroying their vehicle, according to press reports. No one claimed responsibility.

- 19 May in Amludesa, armed militants killed six persons—one magistrate, four police officers, and one civilian—according to press reports. No one claimed responsibility.
- A rocket hit a private residence in Srinagar, injuring six persons, according to press reports. No one claimed responsibility.
- 20 May armed militants threw several bombs at a government vehicle near a bus stop in Srinagar, injuring four police officers and three civilians, according to press reports. No one claimed responsibility.
- 23 May militants fired six grenades at the Civil Secretariat building in Kashmir, which killed one civilian and injuring three others, according to press reports. No one claimed responsibility.
- 2 June a bomb exploded at a religious meeting in Srinagar killing 12 persons and injured seven others, including a senior legislator. The Hizbul-Mujahedin claimed responsibility.
- Press reported unidentified individuals threw a hand grenade into a crowded marketplace in Sopur, injuring 30 civilians and causing major damage. No one claimed responsibility.
- 17 June armed militants shot and injured four civilians in Jammu and Kashmir, according to press reports.
- 30 June a landmine exploded in Srinagar, killing one person, injuring three military personnel and five civilians, damaging several vehicles, and shattering the windows in several nearby hotels, according to press reports. No one claimed responsibility.
- 4 July in Jammu and Kashmir, armed militants killed one person and injured one other, according to press reports. No one claimed responsibility.

- 13 July in Leh, Kashmir, armed militants killed three Buddhist monks, according to press reports. No one claimed responsibility.
- 14 July in the Himalaya Mountains, press reported armed militants attacked two German hikers, killing one and injuring the other. No one claimed responsibility.
- 15 July in Doda, Kashmir, armed militants killed the Doda National Conference district president and his bodyguard. No one claimed responsibility.
- In Srinagar, Kashmir, militants fired nine rifle grenades toward the Civil Secretariat building. The Chief Minister was in his office at the time but was unharmed in the attack, which injured four civilians and damaged two vehicles nearby. The Jaish-e-Mohammed claimed responsibility.
- In Tangmarg, Kashmir, armed militants killed one Indian soldier and one civilian, according to press reports. No one claimed responsibility.
- 24 July a bomb exploded on a private bus in Ballen, killing six persons and injuring 10 others, according to press reports. Kashmiri militants or Sikhs may have been responsible.
- 30 July militants threw a grenade into a crowded market place in Gulmarg, killing one person and injuring five others. No one claimed responsibility.
- 31 July a remote-controlled landmine exploded in Gulmarg, killing one person, injuring five others, and destroying their vehicle, according to press reports. No one claimed responsibility.
- 2 August in Rajwas, armed militants killed 30 persons and injured 47 others when they threw a grenade and then opened fire on a community kitchen, according to press reports. The Lashkar-e-Tayyiba claimed responsibility.
- 10 August a remote-controlled car bomb exploded in Srinagar, killing nine persons, injuring 25 others, and

damaging four cars, according to press reports. Eight police officers were among those killed, and five journalists wounded. No one claimed responsibility.

- 12 August a grenade exploded near a historic mosque in Srinagar, injuring four persons—two Hungarians and two Indians—according to press accounts. No one claimed responsibility.
- 14 August armed militants kidnapped three persons from their residences in Kot Dhara and later killed them. No one claimed responsibility.
- Militants threw a grenade at a bus in Pulwama, injuring 14 passengers. No one claimed responsibility
- 30 September armed militants killed five persons in their private residence in Jammu, according to press reports. No one claimed responsibility.
- 24 November in Akhala, armed militants kidnapped six persons from a bus stop and killed five of them, according to press reports. The fate of the sixth individual was unknown. The Lashkar-e-Toiba was probably responsible.
- 1 December a grenade thrown at a passing security vehicle missed its target and exploded in a crowded street in Pattan injuring 12 persons, according to press reports. No one claimed responsibility.
- Press reported armed militants barged into the private residence of a village defense committee member in Udhampur, killing four children and injuring two others. No one claimed responsibility.
- Militants threw a grenade at a military vehicle in Srinagar, missing their target but injuring three civilians. No one claimed responsibility.
- 6 December a bomb destroyed a vendor's cart, injuring four persons and damaging roadside shops in Muzaffarabad, according to press reporting. No one claimed responsibility.
- 7 December armed militants threw a grenade at a bus

stop in Kupwara, injuring 24 persons, including one special police officer, according to press reports. No one claimed responsibility.

- A bomb exploded near a mosque in Shopian, injuring 31 persons, including three police officers, according to press reports. No one claimed responsibility.
- A bomb exploded in Gohlan, killing a father and injuring his son, according to press reports. No one claimed responsibility.
- 9 December a bomb exploded in Neelum Valley, killing three persons, including a young boy, according to press accounts. No one claimed responsibility.
- 12 December a grenade thrown at an outdoor marketplace in Chadoura injured 12 civilians and four police officers, according to press reports. The Jaish-e-Mohammed was probably responsible.

The Post September-11 Incidents

Maulana Azhar, the founder of Jaish-e-Mohammed organized a suicide car bomb attack outside the Jammu & Kashmir Assembly killing more than thirty people on 1st October, 2001, just a day before Gandhiji's birth day. Jaish-e-Mohammed was also involved in killing more than two hundred people before this incident after its leader Maulana Azhar was released from India in the dawn of twenty-first century. The October incident had serious impact in the minds of Indian people.[16] The Jammu & Kashmir's Chief Minister, Dr. Farooq Abdullah wept in the Assembly of Jammu & Kashmir while addressing to mourn the death of those killed in the militant suicide car bomb attack on the Assembly in Srinagar.

He said : "We are caught between two nations—one perpetrating gruesome violence against our people and another watching, without taking any firm action".[17] Many members of the Assembly were also reportedly wept while the Chief Minister was addressing. This incident in the history of Jammu & Kashmir

Assembly would go in records. Advocating a war against terrorism, Dr. Abdullah stated "if the US could not wait for a day after Black Tuesday of September 11, are not twelve years too much for testing our patience?"[18] In fact, India has been directly being under attack by the Pakistani sponsored terrorism since the early 1980s, during the period when Kashmir has witnessed a number of terrorist attacks. From 1980 to 2000, the terrorist killed thousands of people during that period.

After the incident that took place on 1 October, militants have launched grenade attack on Central Reserve Police Force (CRPF) camps at the Tagore Hall and Indoor Stadium in Srinagar on 13 October 2001. It was reported that two scooter-borne militants were involved in the attack. Both attacks were aimed at disrupting the normal functioning of the government of the Jammu & Kashmir. In fact, the Chief Minister, Mr. Farooq Abdullah, has been repeatedly threatened by the terrorists for his forthright democratic rule and intensified cooperation with Central Government of India for curbing terrorism in the State. In support of terrorist activities, the Pakistani Army on 17 October resorted to heavy firing in the Akhnoor sector in Kashmir immediately after the visit of the US Secretary of Defense, General Colin Powell.[19]

The attack, as expected by the Indian intelligentsia, has facilitated the terrorist filtration into India. Heavy calibre weapons and automatic grenade launchers were used killing innocent people. Pakistan has been encouraging the extremist groups for such destabilizing activities in India from 7 October, the day when the American campaign initiated on Afghanistan. LOC areas such as Kathua wherein Pakistani troops started their activities first and the Mendhar and Akhnoor sectors, the places wherein the Pakistani army posted were made to be very tense. Common people were disturbed in these areas and tension was deliberately created in the Rajouri-Poonch sector.[20] These sectors are strategic in nature. As of the reasons, the Pakistani troops are activating their forces in these areas and trying to create confusion in the minds of the people.

For the last thirty years, Pakistan has been concentrating in the LOC areas by setting up special launching centres code-named Border Action Teams (BAT). The BAT affects people of Pallanwalla area of Akhnoor sector. There are about thirty such camps very active along the LOC from Poonch to Kathua. In these areas, the Indian forces for avoiding infiltration and subversive activities have cleared the bushes known locally as *sarkanda*. Nonetheless, Pakistan refused to accept the report regarding the Pakistani attack in the Akhnoor sector. Its Foreign Office spokesperson Riaz Mohammed Khan stated that there were no any disturbances by Pakistani troops in these areas as reported by the Indian newspapers. He also stated "the dispute in this area is that India wants to fence it, which is against the international law".[21] In the meantime, the terrorist organizations like Jaish-e-Mohammad and Lashkar-e-Taiba have threatened India declaring that they would use more suicide bombers in case India intensify its retaliatory activities in these sectors.

Impact of Terrorism

The terrorist activities have overall impact on society. It creates economic, political and social problems. South Asia, being the leading poor region in the world, is affected more seriously than any other country. In more than sixty years of its independence, Pakistan could not establish a stable and democratic government. India, on the other hand, being big in size and in human resources, could not achieve a political solution for solving the crisis with Pakistan especially referring to issues relating to Jammu and Kashmir, that is the cause for terrorist menace in South Asian region. The people of both the countries are psychologically set against each other, as both the governments' campaign against each other.

In addition, it creates international crisis in this region. For instance, the South Asian countries hesitate in maintaining overt diplomatic relation either with India or Pakistan because the intensity of the conflict faced between these two countries. This is the case with all other countries of the world too. Thus, the world diplomacy is not fully utilised in this region due to continuous problems between India and Pakistan. More than any thing else, the people of the region are affected in all aspects due to terrorist activities. India has lost more than eighty thousand people. Poor people living near border areas are continuously being disturbed. They are not in a position to live in peace. Everyday of their life is under threat due to terrorist acts. Their homes are replaced every now and then. They do not have, therefore, permanent settlements. Education for their kids remains in distant dreams.

The young people are becoming militants, as they are facing these harassments in every walk of their life. In fact, the poor people of these countries are economically affected, as huge amount of money is wasted by either terrorist groups or by the governments themselves. For instance, if all the terrorist camps are closed in Pakistan, the entire region of Pakistan occupied Kashmir (POK) will be emancipated from poverty. Similarly, if the expenditure for fencing the borders and keeping the military forces at borders are diverted for constructive activities in India, the 220 million people now living under poverty line can be lifted in three years.

Studying about the economic impact of terrorism, the World Bank has reported that the attack on WTC on September 11 will have a serious economic impact all over the world. It estimated that developing countries' economic growth fell from 5.5 per cent in 2000 to 2.9 per cent in 2001 and 20,000 to 40,000 children under five years of age were died due to the economic consequences of the attack. It also reported that thousands of children would die worldwide and some 10 million more people will be forced to live below the poverty line in various parts of the world.[22] In this connection it is to be referred that the citizens of the US, the most popular tourists of the world, were under constant fear of travelling in the flights after the incident, which also affected the tourist economy thus creating overall impact in national economy. Most of the aerodromes were seen with number of planes parked due to scarcity of passengers. John F. Kennedy aerodrome has registered with low number of passengers using flights for the first time in the history of its flying experience.

The economic impact would be more serious than ever before if the American campaign against Afghanistan, which started on 7 October 2001, goes on further and further. More campaigning in Afghanistan is going to cost more money that will go against not only the American interest but also the interest of the world in the end. A report notes that the world has witnessed such an economic situation only during the world wars. American economy, as predicted, would face problem in the near future. Due to such economic prediction, the American President appealed in the recent summit of the ASEAN powers in China to note the development in order to assist the process of cleansing up the terrorist camps all over the world.

Fight against the network of Al-Qaeda and Taliban is going to be a tedious and costly process in terms of economy as well as diplomacy.[23] In addition to that, it would also have its own impact in various parts of the world especially in the terrorism prone regions like Middle East and South Asia. According to the US, the counter terrorist action of the world community would have to go by two different phases, cleansing up the network of the Al-Qaeda and Taliban and all other terrorist networks. It is reported that the first phase of American led coalition war would last long for about four years to complete its mission and the second phase will begin after the successful completion of the first phase. It is not clear whether the second phase of war would begin in the South Asian region or elsewhere.

Non-Zero Sum Game

South Asian region is not seriously considered by the US, as India is not given with due place in the American game plan against terrorist networks. Although, the US is proclaiming that it will lead to war against terrorism all over the world, it is not clear in the case of terrorism in South Asia. Moreover, the objective of the first phase—destroying the network of Osama including killing him, is doubtable in nature. Despite of the usages of different sorts of weapons including Cruise missiles, B-2 Stealth bombers, B-52 bombers, Carpet bombs and a number of aircrafts such as C-130 and more than 2,000 bombs, the US could not make much headway in smoking out Bin Laden. Moreover, the US interest is not very clear about dealing with the linkages of the Al-Qaeda as well as the Taliban forces in the future.

Whether the US would include the war against connected terrorist activities in different regions including South Asia in the first phase itself or it would deal it separately is not very clear. However, its interest in extending war was noticed when the American government had reportedly issued a statement which revealed its plan for attacking Somalia. Nonetheless, the Indian Government changed its position stating that it did not want anyone's help to deal with the South Asian terrorist especially the terrorist in the Jammu & Kashmir Valley. The American participation in the fight against terrorism in this region, however, cannot be ruled out.

Either the Indian or the Pakistani perception on terrorism is not agreed by the US unlike France, China, Germany, Japan and Russia. In the case of Russia, it is very vocal in support of Indian position. It should be noted in ASEAN summit held in October 2001 in which the US also participated, the host country, China has rendered unexpected support to India. The German chancellor also supported the Indian stance in dealing with terrorism in South Asian Region. Although the US has shown interest recently to accommodate India in the UN Security Council as a permanent member, it is to be seen whether it will agree with the Indian perception or the Pakistani perception on issues relating to terrorism. The important point to be noted with concern here is that Pakistan keeps its perception in view that the terrorist in the Valley are freedom fighters.

The US considers Pakistan as a frontline partner in the US led coalition war. For, it awarded with economic boon apart from the morale boost for its foreign policy, which is very much a matter for a nation in its long run. A liberal economic package, including debt relief and immediate assistance of about 600 million dollars to Pakistan, for example, is helping Pakistan to carry out major plans against India in an amazing way. It is doubted that the money may be spent for supporting terrorists in Jammu and Kashmir. However, the decision to use the amount for educational reform by President, Pervez Musharraf was well appreciated, as it was a long bending one in the politically unstable Pakistan for more than twenty-five years. It should also be noted that the then President General Zia-ul-Huq initiated the reform process during his period. Contrary to Musharraf's interest, the development in Pakistan may disturb the reform process and certain groups closely associated with government as well as terrorist groups may misuse it. Such situation may further help the fundamentalist for campaigning against President Musharraf's initiatives as well as India's diplomatic initiative for establishing peaceful relation with Pakistan. However, President Obama may change the course of diplomacy in South Asia.

The Game of Pakistan

Pakistan has been playing double role in the fight against global terrorism. In one way, as it is well known, it has been encouraging various subversive activities of the terrorists in the Kashmir Valley and in another way it has been promising to Americans that it would fight against the network of Al-Qaeda and Osama Bin Laden. Of all the forty countries that came forward for helping the US in its endeavour, Pakistan was seriously considered by the US not just because of its geographical proximity with Afghanistan but because of its friendship with both the Talibans and Bin Laden groups. The bold and unimaginable initiative of Musharraf came off shaking the ISI Chief who was close to the fundamentalist forces and whom the General believed with for managing the countries' serious political affairs. Surprisingly again, he has given a key position to Mr. Gen. Ehsan-ul-Huq who belongs to Pashthun ethnic group. It is to be noted that Pashthun comprises forty per cent of the Afghan population. Nevertheless, as mentioned above, Musharraf might face serious problems in the future due to growing civilian supports to both Taliban and Osama Bin Laden groups. Only the American or the Government of India can help Pakistan in a crisis when the terrorists group establishes such a network with civilian population affecting the normal functioning of the government in the years to come.

For crisis management, it is reported that Pakistan is planning to have one more Kargil like war with India. According to the security planners of Pakistan, it is more important in order to suppress the overwhelming support of the people to Osama Bin Laden. The Jihad groups are also reportedly interested to overthrow any government. The disruption in Pakistan has gone to the extent of seeking the American help to safeguard the nuclear facilities and the reputedly available twenty-four nuclear bombs, which may fall in the hands of terrorists. More than twenty Pakistani terrorists were killed in the American campaign in Afghanistan. Even then, Pakistan maintained that it had nothing to do with the terrorists killed in Afghanistan and it claimed that it never helped any subversive activities in the ongoing war against international terrorism. It is to be mentioned here that the Pakistani military had supplied weapons to militants to involve in subversive activities in Jammu & Kashmir during the period of early phase of American war in Afghanistan.

As coverage, therefore, it may prepare war as the best resort to come out of all the internal problems including the problems relating to the influx of refugees. It is estimated that more than three million people from Afghanistan were camped in Pakistan as refugees.[24] Although Pakistan played foul game in the American campaign against Afghanistan, it could use the situation for its advantage. General Musharraf played, many noted, appreciable role in positioning Pakistan in a more advanced level of diplomatic relation not only with the US but also with India. The entire team of Pakistani diplomats was appreciated for such an able management of crisis in October 1999, which had a direct bearing for internal security of South Asian region . As expected, the American campaign in South Asia under Obama leadership may succeed further.

Old Politics in the New World

Although the lifting of the US sanction may benefit India in the long run, it is believed that it will not serve the strategic interest of India in the coming years as there are some more hurdles on the ways of scientific co-operation between these two countries. More importantly, the position given to Pakistan in the fight against global terrorism would, as many in India think, jeopardize the Indian interests in the world politics. It should be remembered that India has been proposing to fight against terrorism in the world for more than a decade now. Such genuine role, as noted by many in India, is not respected by the US. Being the country that has solid experience in fighting against terrorists, India could have been very well involved fully in the process going on in Afghanistan. The geographical proximity of Pakistan should not be the only point that has to be considered in the fight against terrorist groups.[25] In fact, the US wants to engage the old politics in the new world. In the 1990s, the US was very reluctant to accept Indian proposal for fighting against terrorists. US did not consider such proposal of India in the UN. Rather, it was advocating different means for countering the global terrorists differing from Indian position. If US could have agreed upon the proposal, terrorism might have been to some extent wiped out by now and the US could have averted the September 11 incident, which led for cycle of incidents in the South Asian region. Let it be the way the American decides on the global fight against terrorism now.

On 6 October 2001 the visiting British Prime Minister Mr. Tony Blair in Delhi indirectly indicated that India should not worry too much thinking about US led coalition and the Pakistan's position in it. Instead, according to him, India should think of developing a good strategic rapport with Pakistan using this occasion so as to resolve the conflict in Jammu & Kashmir. In that connection he stated to his Indian counterpart that UK's relationship with Pakistan after the military coup in October 1999 is not at the cost of India at this moment when global terrorism is dealt in totality.[26] As he noted that India was a strategic partner in the fight against global terrorism and Pakistan was a tactical partner specifically in dealing with Taliban and Bin Laden forces. Nonetheless, India should advantageously utilize the opportunity rather than be critical against Pakistan and the US.

As a diplomatic gesture, the UK had already banned the Jaish-e-Mohammad (JeM) and Lashkar-e-Taiba (LeT) that were very active in Jammu and Kashmir.[27] The British gesture to ban these organizations was appreciated by many diplomats not only in India but also in many countries of South Asia. The Sri Lankan government welcomed the British initiative and stated such effort of UK would help the South Asian countries to achieve peace. The US did not decide to include these organizations in its ban list of Foreign Terrorist Organizations (FTO) The FTO only designates twenty-three organizations. In the list of the UK, in addition to the twenty-three organizations, JeM and JeT are included. However, both the US and UK did not accept the Indian report that Pakistan has been sponsoring terrorism in South Asia, especially against India and it has connection with international terrorist network.[28] The list of prominent Foreign Terrorist Organization (FTO) is noted below :

- Abu Nidal Organization (ANO)
- Abu Sayyaf Group (ASG)
- Armed Islamic Group (GIA)
- Aum Shinriykyo

- Basque Fatherland and Liberty (ETA)
- HAMAS (Islamic Resistance Movement)
- Harakat ul-Mujahidin (HUM)
- Hizballah (Party of God)
- Gama'a al-Islamiyya (Islamic Group, IG)
- Japanese Red Army (JRA)
- al-Jihad
- Kach
- Kahane Chai
- Kurdistan Workers' Party (PKK)
- Liberation Tigers of Tamil Elam (LTTE)
- Mujahedin-e Khalq Organization (MEK, MKO, NCR, and many others)
- National Liberation Army (ELN)
- Palestine Islamic Jihad–Shaqaqi Faction (PIJ)
- Palestine Liberation Front–Abu Abbas Faction (PLF)
- Popular Front for the Liberation of Palestine (PFLP)
- Popular Front for the Liberation of Palestine–General Command (PFLP-GC)
- al-Qa'ida
- Revolutionary Armed Forces of Colombia (FARC)
- Revolutionary Organization 17 November (17 November)
- Revolutionary People's Liberation Army/Front (DHKP/C)
- Revolutionary People's Struggle (ELA)
- Shining Path (Sendero Luminoso, SL)
- Tupac Amaru Revolutionary Movement (MRTA)

It is disappointing to note that both the US and UK are silent in the face of the argument of Pakistan that claims both the groups involved in terrorist acts in the Valley are freedom fighters. On 13 October 2001, the Union Home Minister Mr. L.K. Advani said that the country had drawn world attention to Pakistan's sponsorship of terrorism as a state policy and there were direct connections between the forces of the WTC attack and the forces that have been destabilizing the Indian sub-continent, especially in the Jammu & Kashmir region.[29] The developments in the South Asian region, although monitored by the Americans very carefully, are not seriously considered. The American President George Bush noted in September immediately after the WTC attack that the US believed Pakistan more than any other country in Asia.[30] It is, therefore, very clear that the US is interested to maintain its friendship with Pakistan, which has been close to US for more than fifty years now. In its game plan, it gives more priority to Pakistan than any other countries in South Asian region. Thus, the US does not like to alter the South Asian diplomatic situation that was prevailing during the period of cold war.

However, it was given with the impression during the visit of the former President Clinton that the US would prepare to go along with India rather than with Pakistan. Many people in the sub-continent, if not very exclusive, thought that Pakistan would drop its hold with the US and new turn of political events both in the region as well as in the world would emerge. President Clinton addressed the Indian audience as if the US was heading to such eventuality preparing to develop new relationship with India in the new millennium. Nevertheless, all went in dismay. As of the reason, Pakistan has once again become good friend of the US in the new world and it is hoped that their friendship would last long for ever. Thus, the old politics in the new world has begun for the first time in this century in the South Asian region.

The latest developments, never expected by many in the recent past, have happened just because of the September 11 incident in the US. Drawing the enthusiasm in this process, the Pakistani diplomats went to the extent of utilizing the American homecoming to their maximum especially in the case of dealing with conflicts faced with India.[31] In this connection, Mr. Riaz Mohammad Khan stated that Pakistan would stick to position taken during the cold war period on Kashmir issues. It should be noted that during that period the UN Security Council resolutions passed a resolution acknowledging Kashmir as dangerous source of conflict between India and Pakistan. It also stressed on the rights for self-determination by the people of Jammu & Kashmir. Since it is remaining unimplemented, as noted by him, the process should start now for self-determination of people of Kashmir.[32] India, however, remains firm in its commitment on the question of Kashmir, which is considered to be the integral part, and play the self-restraint policy without minding to the cold war politics of US in this new millennium.

Conclusion

The overwhelming support of the international community including many Islamic nations of West Asia for combating terrorism and the American role against Pakistan's terrorist groups are welcome signs to the new world of twenty first century. The coalition leader, the US, should properly utilize this opportunity. If not, the chance may be lost forever. Therefore, a serious effort in defining the concept should be explored by reasonably considering the interest of every nation. As India has been demanding for quite some time, an international conference on terrorism should be organized for deciding on various issues relating to the problems of encountering the global terrorism. Instruments of international law, especially dealing with extradition agreements among world nations, should be strengthened. Countries capable of effective cooperation in the process should not be neglected by the US. Especially India should be given a due place in the coalition arrangement for successfully carrying out the mission, as it has signed extradition treaty with twelve important countries in the world including the one signed with Spain in June 2002. Thus, effective collision arrangement against international terrorism would not only help eradicate terrorism in the world but also to eradicate poverty. India, being an aspirer to become one of the developed nations by 2020, will be greatly benefited.

NOTES

1. For more information on the history and the network of terrorism, see the website *http//www.terrorism.com*

2. *Ibid.*
3. *United Nations News Letter* (New Delhi), Vol. 56, Number 40, 6 Oct. to 12 Oct., 2001, pp. 3–4
4. For more details on the concept see K. Prabha, *Terrorism : An Instrument of Foreign Policy* (New Delhi: South Asian Publishers, 2000), pp. 13–43
5. *Ibid.*
6. *Ibid.*
7. See the website, No. 1
8. *Ibid.*
9. *Ibid.*
10. K. Prabha, Terrorism : An Instrument of Foreign Policy, No.4. p. 127; See also Parama Sinha Palit, "*The Kashmir Policy of the United States : A Study of the Perceptions*, Conflicts and Dilemmas", *Strategic Analyses* (New Delhi), Vol. XXV, No. 6, Sept. 2001, pp. 781–783
11. *Ibid.*
12. *Ibid.,* for more detail on population, see Amaury de Riencourt, "India and Pakistan in the Shadow of Afghanistan", *Foreign Affairs* (New York), Vol. 62, No. 2, Winter1982/83, pp. 416–417.
13. *Ibid.* p. 144
14. *The Hindu* (Chennai), Oct. 9, 2001.
15. *Ibid.,* See also the website, No.1.
16. *Indian Express* (Chennai), Oct. 2, 2001.
17. *Ibid.*
18. *The Hindu,* Oct. 19, 2001
19. *Ibid.*
20. *Ibid.*
21. *The Hindu,* Oct. 15, 2001.
22. *Ibid.*
23. *UN Newsletter,* No. 3, p. 5
24. *Ibid.*
25. *The Hindu,* Oct.7, 2001.
26. *Ibid.*
27. *Ibid.*
28. See Parama Sinha Palit, *The Kashmir Policy of the United States*, No. 10.
29. *Ibid.*
30. *Ibid.*
31. *Indian Express*, Oct. 24, 2001.
32. *Ibid.*

Chapter **- 4**

The Issues of Human Rights

"Violence is the way of barbarians; non-violence is the way of men" —Mahatma Gandhi

"Blessed are the peacemakers, for they shall be called the children of God" —Mathew 5:9 (New Testament)

"When I gave food to the poor, they called me a saint, when I asked why the poor were hungry, they called me a communist" —Dom Helder Camara, Brazilian Archbishop

Introduction

Human rights movements are considered to be part and parcel of peace movements. There are more than thirty thousand organizations working for the objective of promoting human rights today. India is one of the leading countries in the world that has majority number of non-governmental organizations (NGOs) registered for the purpose. Almost all the NGOs receive financial support from the affluent western countries. Since the early 1970s, the US has been leading in helping the maximum number of such organizations. Only in the mid 1980s, human rights movements have become popular in India. During the cold war period, intellectuals of developing countries argued against the American methods of promoting this concept. According to them, the Americans used the concept of human rights as coverage for curtailing economic aids to developing countries. It was also argued that instead of helping the deserving poor countries, the Americans imposed certain legalities in the pretext of promoting human rights. As a result, many countries were denied of the help not only from US but also from all other developed countries.[1] Thus, it was obligatory on the part of the recipients to adopt human rights standard for receiving help from donor countries.

The American diplomats have also used the concept of human rights in the context to arms cortrol agreements. For example, the Strategic Arms Limitation Talks (SALT) of 1970s can be noted. In fact, during the period of SALT negotiation, the US blamed the former Soviet Union for not having followed the human rights standard. Because of such response of the US in linking up the human rights issues even in the arms control agreement like SALT, the process of finding solution for curbing the long-range (strategic) nuclear missiles were delayed. The same tactics were also adopted in the case of Intermediate Nuclear Forces (INF) agreements in the 1980s that had aimed at banning all short-range missiles deployed in the former West and Eastern Europe. China was also blamed of human rights violation and accordingly being denied of the economic help of the US during the period of cold war between the superpowers.

History of Human Rights

The UN was established on 24 October 1945 for achieving international peace and development based on the principles of justice, human dignity and the well-being of all people. The "fundamental human rights" is the second item in the preamble to the Charter of the UN. For achieving the second item of the UN Charter, on December 10 1948, the UN produced the Universal Declaration of Human Rights (UDHR) aiming at protecting individual citizens from abuses. It states that human rights are the formation of freedom, justice and peace in the world. The United States (US), being the leader of democracy and forerunner in recognizing the rights of individual citizens, was very active in promoting and advancing human right activities all over the world. It funded thousands of individuals and organizations to work upon the UN's objectives.[2] In fact, it helped people coming from Europe fearing Hitler. For instance, Albert Einstein was given with political asylum along with his fellow friends, Strassman and Henry, who had escaped from Germany during the period of Second Word War. It should be noted that at that point of time the nuclear research was at its peak and Einstein advocated the theory of $E=Mc^2$. Although Einstein helped produce atomic bombs—little boy and fat man, which were used by the US against the Japanese cities, Hiroshima and Nagasaki on 6 and 9 August 1945 respectively, he had turned out to be a great peace-maker and advocate of human rights in 1950s. He formed up Pugwash (name of a village in Canada) movement for the cause of serving world peace and devoted his precious part of his life for the cause of human rights.

In US, the former first lady, Eleanor Roosevelt, was devoting her time and energy for the cause of women's rights and for the rights of minorities. She had, in fact, skilfully negotiated with various world leaders between 1945 to 1948 for promotion of human rights officially by the US apart from the UN, the newly formed up international organization at that time. Thousands of NGOs all over the world wrote letters appreciating the first lady and promised her of their consistent support. One of the leading Pan-American Human Rights (PAHR) movement conferences in Mexico was very determined to human rights activities from Latin American region. In the US, the American Jewish Committee, (JC) National Council of Churches (NCC) and the Commission to Study the Organization of Peace (CSOP) had supported relentlessly Eleanor Roosevelt.[3] Thousands of NGOs had requested even to the extent that the US Government should back out from the UN if the UN did not adopt human rights charter. Eminent scientists, industrialists and philanthropists had campaigned among congressional representatives in the White House along with Mrs. Roosevelt. Being the first lady, she could succeed in generating both public and government support. Finally, the concept was officially recognized.[4]

Thus, for the first time in the history of peace, the human

rights regulation was set according to general human standard. Extensive analysis of the concept was done and regulations were written accordingly under her leadership. In fact, personally she took the pain of writing the draft of the Universal Declaration of Human Rights (UDHR) to be adopted by the UN General Assembly (UNGA).[5] Thus, it was successfully adopted by the UNGA on 10 December 1948, a day now celebrated throughout the world as Human Rights Day. Some of the important events that formed the basis of UDHR are noted below:[6]

- On 26 June 1945, the Charter of the United Nations and Statute of the International Court of Justice, in San Francisco was singed;
- On 21 June 1946, Commission on Human Rights under Economic and Social Council resolution 9 (II), and Commission on the Status of Women under resolution 11 (II) of the Economic and Social Council were established;
- 9 December 1948, the General Assembly of the Convention adopted a resolution on the Prevention and Punishment of the Crime of Genocide;
- 10 December1948, the General Assembly of the Universal Declaration of Human Rights was adopted;
- On 2 December1949, the General Assembly of the Convention adopted resolution for the Suppression of the Traffic in Persons and of the Exploitation of the Prostitution of Others;
- On 4 November 1950, the members of the Council of Europe of the Convention adopted a resolution for the Protection of Human Rights and Fundamental Freedoms (European Convention on Human Rights);
- On 1 December 1950, the Committee on Crime Prevention and Control under General Assembly Resolution 415 (V) was created;
- On 28 July 1951, a resolution was Adopted by a United Nations Conference of Plenipotentiaries of the Convention relating to the Status of Refugees;

- On 20 December 1952, the General Assembly of the Convention adopted a resolution on the Political Rights of Women;
- On 23 October 1953, the General Assembly of the Protocol adopted resolution for amending the Slavery Convention signed at Geneva on 25 September 1926;
- On 28 September1954, a Conference of Plenipotentiaries of the Convention adopted a resolution relating to the Status of Stateless Persons;
- On 30 August 1955, the First United Nations Congress adopted resolution on the Prevention of Crime and the Treatment of Offenders of the Standard Minimum Rules for the Treatment of Prisoners;
- On 7 September 1956, a resolution was adopted by a Conference of Plenipotentiaries of the Supplementary Convention on the Abolition of Slavery, the Slave Trade, and Institutions and Practices Similar to Slavery;
- On 29 January 1957, a resolution was adopted by the General Assembly of the Convention on the Nationality of Married Women;
- On 25 June 1957, a resolution was adopted by the General Conference of the International Labour Organization of the Convention on the Abolition of Forced Labour;
- On 30 July 1959, a resolution was adopted by the Economic and Social Council of Resolution 728 F (XXVIII), giving the Commission on Human Rights certain responsibilities with regard to the treatment of communications dealing with human rights;
- On 20 November 1959, a resolution was adopted by the General Assembly of the Declaration of the *Rights of the Child* ;
- On 14 December 1960, a resolution was adopted by the General Assembly of the Declaration on the *Granting of Independence to Colonial Countries and Peoples;* and

- On 30 August 1961, a resolution was adopted Conference of Plenipotentiaries of the Convention on the Reduction of Statelessness.

The UDHR was signed in 1960s and came into force in 1976 when most of the countries signed the UDHR had ratified it. It should be noted that UDHR is only a code of standard not of law. It says that "all people are born free and equal in dignity and rights and that they should not be discriminated against because of their nationality, ethnicity, religion, race, gender, political opinion, wealth or property." Some of the rights spelled out in the declaration are:[7]

- Freedom from slavery;
- Freedom from torture;
- Equal protection of the law, freedom from arbitrary arrest and the Right to a fair trial;
- Freedom of thought, opinion, religion and expression;
- The right to education;
- The right to an adequate standard of living, including good health;
- Shelter and enough food: and
- The right to work and to form and join trade unions.

Critical Analysis of the Concept

The concept of human rights is viewed in various ways. Some people view it in relation to the concept of 'duty' and some do not. According to them, rights and duties are part in human endeavour. Without duty or action rights cannot be demanded.[8] Similarly without rights, duty cannot be carried out in a given condition. According to Oxford Dictionary, right is defined as 'something one is entitled to' and duty is defined as 'action required by a particular person'. Although they are complementary to each other, the Charter gives importance only to the concept of right not to the concept of duty. Eleanor

Roosevelt herself noted once that the human right movements should help the helpless all over the world. When the initiative in helping them out succeeds, according to her, the duty and responsibility can be noted with concern.[9] Born with the idea of promoting the rights of people for freedom from all sorts of suffering, the concept should never be understood by unnecessary highlights on duty. A Roman philosopher Seneca expressed in this context over 2,000 years ago: "...hungry people listen not to reason nor cares for justice, nor is bent by a prayer". Working among such level of poor people needs devotion of love.[10]

Nonetheless, intellectuals supporting the concept of duty in relation to the promotion of human rights argue that the rights can only be claimed when a duty is performed. When one performs a duty, certain methodologies have to be adopted for completing it. Such methodology is the right of that particular duty without which it cannot be duty.[11] Therefore, duty is a right related act. Similarly, right is a duty related act. They are, therefore, inseparable. If a person wants to enjoy the rights, he or she should perform the duty for receiving or achieving such rights. Through prayer, only blessing of God can be obtained. Thus, without any action, it is not possible to attain anything. It is, therefore, important to realize both the concepts in relation to promotion of human rights.[12] However, it should be noted here that depending upon the situation, it has to be employed by adopting flexible strategy for promoting human rights.

In this connection, the UN General Assembly resolution 217A (III) of 10 December 1948 refers to duty in relation to carry out the human right activities by activists of human rights. It does stress upon the obligation or duty of the person in need of rights.[13] For example, Article 29 notes that "everyone has duties to the community in securing due recognition and respect for the rights and freedoms of others and of meeting the just requirements of morality, public order and the general welfare in a democratic society".[14] Thus, a necessary condition is set for the human right activists in order to serve the very spirit of the UN Charter for world peace. Unnecessary botheration on duty will confuse the minds of people. If food is not taken, energy cannot be generated. The right is like a food. That has to be served first.

Moreover, many scholars argue that the duty cannot be taken into consideration in the same vein, while promoting the rights of the deprived people of the world who suffer without basic amenities for their day-to-day life. Therefore, the human rights activists, inspite of wasting much time on the concept, should help to acquire the required amenities for poor people. Nevertheless, according to them, the concept of duty can be advanced gradually later on when the beneficiaries expand their activities by enjoying the required rights. Thus, for them, the rights for survival with basic amenities do not represent duty at all. If it does, as they note, that should be neglected by understanding about the necessary condition.

Nonetheless, confusion prevails still among people in understanding the very basis of the concept. For avoiding such confusion, it is necessary to note the teachings of Ramakrishna Paramahamsa who notes that man should strive in controlling his mind while serving the humanity. According to him, confusion prevails once when one strives for material benefit out of his or her service. Service, therefore, needs 'mahatma'—the great soul that expects no return including love. Such attitude is needed for human right activists. In addition, the school of thought of Thomas Paine, the great American political philosopher, notes in his popular book, *The Rights of Man about the Moral Obligation of a Person in relation to his Duty or Action*. To this effect, the article 30 of the UDHR declares, "nothing in this declaration may be interpreted as implying for any state, group or person any right to engage in any activity or to perform any act aimed at the destruction of any of the rights and freedoms set forth herein".[15] Therefore, a heart-oriented approach is more relevant than mind-oriented for service related activities. HR is service related not duty related.

Youth and Human Rights

The fundamental principles of democratic society based on respect for human dignity should be taught among younger generation of the world in order to achieve the Universal Declaration of Human Rights. Therefore, promotion of HR activities among them has to be intensified and concern individuals and organization should give them with proper advice and guidelines to carry out activities in respective nations. At present more than two billion youngsters are available all over the word. Accordingly, the UN should devise plans and motivate them. Without their participation, it is impossible to achieve the objectives of UDHR.[16] In fact, practical steps in attracting young people were initiated by organizing fellowship and scholarship programmes in various educational institutions of the world in 1846 when the first voluntary organization, the world Evangelist Alliance, was formed for the cause of eradicating religious exploitation. There are now millions of young people ageing from 18 to 35 working for the cause of peace all over the world. Most of their activities are centered on the following areas.[17]

- Administration of Justice;
- International law and human rights;
- Exchanging national capacity;
- Minorities and indigenous people;
- Racism and racial discrimination;
- HIV/AIDS Migrant workers;
- Religious intolerance, children, women and slavery;
- Economic social and cultural rights; and
- Civil, Political Rights and Rights to Development.

By working together, they have been contributing to achieve the goal of the UN to accomplish international peace. As the HR activity is one of the complimentary and central one for the cause of world peace, it is important to expand and develop it. In this respect, Eleanor Roosevelt once stated that "basically we could not have peace, or an atmosphere in which peace could grow, unless we recognized the rights of individual human beings… their importance, their dignity…and agreed that was the basic thing that had to be accepted throughout the world".[18] Thus, she recognizes individual human rights as a pertinent one for achieving world peace. Rather, it can be stated that it is pre-condition. Otherwise, the effort in promotion of peace through UN will not succeed.

For her, individual peace is as important as national as well as international peace. If a person is not treated with dignity, he is bound to be indifferent to the society. As a human being, he has to enjoy like others. If he or she is deprived of the rights that others are enjoying, he or she will become violent. Therefore, as she notes, individual dignity is important. Such understanding on individual rights should be uniformly accepted by the nations of the world and accordingly law should be enacted for management of such individual peace. Violators of the individual dignity should be brought into book and punished appropriately. A nation should take this matter as very important and holy and abide by acting truthfully. Terrorism is, therefore, the creation of a society that does not respect the dignity of fellowmen. This is the case with any form of violence such a revolution, extremism, fanaticism, radicalism, intolerance, discrimination, chauvinism, bigotry, prejudice, intolerance, etc.

In India, individual dignity, as many agree, is at constant stake. Because of the social system, individuals are not treated equally. Such situation will not help establish peace in local level. As a result, national peace may not be feasible. When a nation is not protecting individual peace, it does not truly exist. Nation should constitutionally guarantee every individual the right of enjoying the dignity as human being. Such rights should also be protected in a crisis period. If not, everything will be meaningless. In this context, the third and popular General Secretary of the UN, Mr. U. Thant, made an important observation when he was requested to talk about HR among young people in 1977. He said, "the world has come to a clear realization of the fact that freedom, justice and world peace can only be assured through the international promotion and protection of individual rights".[19] Directing the youths with rights, intention may help achieve the objectives. Since India is a leading country in possession of youth population, it can ably direct the youths towards establishing egalitarian society by way of promoting human rights in general and individual dignity in particular.

Human Rights Violation

Although millions of people are working to promote and protect the human rights, a foolproof protection appears to be impossible because of the existing social, political and economic situation of respective countries.[20] The situation in some of the developing and Least Developing Countries (LDC) are pathetic due to poverty. More than two billion people recorded to be living under poverty having less than one dollar a day in the world are majority in number in Africa. HR situation in Latin America and Asia, although different from Africa, is not encouraging.[21] In developed countries, human rights are violated due to affluence that leads for uneven human development. For instance, in US, the life style of the white people cannot be compared with Black people.[22] Such uneven economic development violates the rights of individuals in US.

In addition, almost in all developed countries like US, UK, France and Germany, certain level of racial discrimination exist, which is directly violating the human rights. Because of the colour, as in the case of caste in India, the black people are not equally treated. Religious intolerance also prevails in developed countries. For instance, recently in Iraq, the American soldiers harassed the Muslims prisoners in jail like animals violating the law of war in general and human rights in particular. Some of the HR violations are noted below.[23]

- More than one million children, mostly girls, are forced into prostitution every year;

- Disabled persons constituting ten per cent of the world's population are not facilitated socially, economically and politically;
- 79 per cent of the indigenous people in Peru are neglected and not adequately facilitated by the government. Half of them live in extreme poverty;
- Some 250 million children between the age group of 5 to 14 are currently working, according to the International Labour Office (ILO). Of this total, 120 million children are working full-time; 61 per cent of child workers (153 million) are found in Asia; 32 per cent in Africa; and 7 per cent in Latin America;
- 2 million girls each year are at risk of genital mutilation (approximately 6,000 girls per day);
- 160 million children are moderately or severely malnourished and 110 million are out of school;
- At least 500,000 children a year are left motherless by death in childbirth. Over 1.3 billion people in developing countries live with less than one dollar per day ; and,
- Women compromising 70 per cent of the world's poor are not treated equally.

Women and Human Rights

Women are the most affected humankinds in the world. They are not being treated equally. They make up one-third of the total labour force in the world. Nonetheless, the wage they receive for the same work done by men is 30 to 40 per cent less than men. Because of this discrimination, their health condition is deteriorated. A research report notes that in Asia the boys under 5 years of age receive 16 per cent more food than girls.[24] It is the condition in the educational field too. For every three illiterate women in the world there are two literate men. In addition, it is estimated that one-third of the world's households are headed by women in the world. The list of discrimination against women is expanding when one looks at their pathetic condition in politics, which is the closest domain in decision-making process. Only 4.1 per cent of the world's cabinet ministers were women and 77 countries had no women ministers in the world.[25]

As of the reason, the fourth conference convened in Beijing, China in 1995, concluded by urging the world communities work for promoting the UDHR referring to the "inherent dignity and equal rights of all members of the human race..." For, it recommended that women community of the world should be brought into decision-making positions in government and other institutions.[26] Recently, the world March of Woman 2000 was held in New York City in which nearly 6,000 organizations around the world participated for the elimination of poverty and violence against women. It was organized because of the enthusiasm drawn by the earlier marches held in Morocco where 5,00,000 people had participated chanting, "We share the earth, let's share the wealth".[27]

Similarly, in Haiti—the city of Democratic Republic of Congo—popular slogan such as "Day without women" was raised by sizable number of participants in the strike. In front of World Trade Organization (WTO) in Geneva and in Brazil and in front of Sao Paola Stock Exchange, women volunteers of the entire world organized great demonstrations. Thus, the women of the world have proved that they are capable of fighting for their rights and they will never remain calm in the face of provocation by men of their respective countries. Some of the facts exposed about suffering of women around the world by these movements are: [28]

- Egyptian governments did not allow sufficient amount in its budget, rather the amount is reduced for facilitating the health care of the women who were equally participating in the production process;
- In Uganda, women were forced to cultivate or farm on bush or on hilly terrain; and

- In Zimbabwe 20 per cent of the women, who were affected by HIV positive were neglected.

The Plight of Women in India

In India, the HR situation in relation to women is not encouraging as the woman folks are not equal in social, economic and political fronts. Recently, the fight for 30 per cent reservation has picked up momentum. However, men, especially the political leaders, were thwarting it repeatedly. Subversive acts against women continue in India as usual. It is a quite heartening to note that almost 80 per cent of the women in India are engaged in agricultural work. For their labour, they get meagre wage. Women attend more than 90 per cent of the home work.[29] The husbands of Indian women are known for their maltreatment and physical abuse of their partners in the world. They keep the women in houses without giving them fundamental freedom. As a result, the women suffering from mental diseases are more in number.

During the pregnancy period, they are also harassed and not given proper medical attention. In case, if they bear female child, they are looked down, as if they are only responsible for such act. The truth, however, is that only the men are responsible for female or male child and not the women. Even this small fact is not known or deliberately neglected in India. Highly educated males are also irresponsibly hiding the truth and some time they blame God for bearing female child. Women in India also do the grooming work of the child throughout their life, as mothers and grandmothers. Men spare only little time for this important task.[30] In the educational process of the children too, women's participate fully. Even the educated women in India are helpless and they are subjective for harassment by their men. The working women in government or private firms and companies are much abused in their work places. They are maltreated and sexually harassed.

Political leaders are unmindful of the situation. Even they

do not give much support for the existing law for protecting women. It is reported that political leaders in India have many wives illegally. Law is blind in their cases. Women's representation in political parties is very less. As a result, they are helpless in promotion of their political rights. Economically, they are dependent of their men. Even if they earn, they are deprived of taking any economic decision on their own. Thus women in India live as a submissive human beings. The human right activists should extend their helping hand and fight for empowerment of woman folks in India.[31] The Indian universities should start more studies relating to women problems. Educating women is the only way that will put in at par with men in the turn of this new century.

Poverty and Human Rights

Of all the challenges, poverty is the most important one, as more than two billion out of six billion population of the world live under poverty. Poverty is endemic in almost all the third world countries. As stated above, the African, Latin American and Asian countries are leading in number of poverty ridden people in the world. South Asia is one of the leading regions in poverty. Bangladesh is worst affected in this syndrome. Similarly, Nepal and Bhutan are also trailing behind in raising the standard of living of their respective people. Sri Lanka, Pakistan and India, although improved in certain lines of economic measurement, are not appreciable in their scheme of developing poverty prone people. India is having the majority number of people living below poverty line in the world. As of the reason, the situation for human rights promotion is worst in this part of the world. African and Latin American countries are also in the same condition. African countries are, especially West African countries, are comparatively very bad.

Mother Teresa once stated that, "the biggest disease today is not leprosy or tuberculosis, but the lack of love and charity, the terrible indifference towards one's neighbour who lives at the roadside assaulted by exploitation, corruption and poverty".[32] Poverty, the centre of many evils should be abolished, or else it will not only abolish the peace among people in certain regions but also peace among nations. Therefore, HR activists should concentrate in attacking poverty by intensifying their help to the helpless. For example in India alone, it is estimated that 135 million people have no access to basic health facilities, 226 million are not accessible for safe drinking water and about 70 per cent of the population lack basic sanitation facilities. As 75 per cent of the world "thorium" is located in India, the largest number of diseased, disabled and blind people of the world is also available only in India. It is to be noted that 52 per cent of the people of India earn only one dollar a day and strive to live.[33]

HR activists of India should be more responsible in their work and try to help eradicating poverty among people first. India should succeed in its effort with the support of the UN and related HR organizations including NGOs. The UN millennium goals, which are accepted by 189 countries, for eradicating poverty in the world by 2015 must be meticulously carried on with the interest of promoting both individuals and HR rights in various countries, especially the poor countries of the world. India's position in the human development record is poor even after 62 years of its independence as one looks at the statistics given by a team of doctors working in Delhi along with the volunteers of World Health Organization (WHO). It states that "every five seconds one person goes blind in the world and a child goes every minute. There are 18.6 million estimated blinds in India". It continues that "India has the largest blind population in the world. There are about one million blind children in India. Most of that blindness can be removed if children simply wore spectacles".[34]

The scenario on poverty all over the world is more serious than ever before. More than 70 per cent of the poor people of the world are living in the developing countries. Because of poverty, millions of people do not get education in the world.

Only 950 million adults, out of 6 billion of total population of the present world, are branded to be literate. Billions of them do not have sufficient food, shelter, drinking water, employment, health care and educational facilities. In the contrary, the world spends one trillion dollars per year for military activities, almost 2,00,0000 dollars a minute and contributes only 0.7 per cent of the GNP as aid to the UN for peace and development activities per year. Even the minimum share 0.01 per cent is not fully paid by many countries today. A rich country like the US also does not pay its due regularly.[35] Unfortunately, therefore, the UN is often close to bankruptcy.

Conclusion

Human Right activists all over the world have to work together and consolidate the peace movements as a whole. They should not fall prey to politics or any other stakes. Forgetting about the differences, all countries of the world should help the activists by providing sufficient funds in order to help the helpless poor people. All the promoters of HR should play, therefore, positive role without confusion especially on understanding the very concept. Women and children of the world have to be considered by the activists first and they should be helped with conviction. Activities in Africa, Asia, Latin America and other deserving regions of the world have to be intensified. More importantly, they should effectively utilize the Information and Communication Technology (ICT) for promotion of human rights in a faster way.

NOTES

1. See the United Nations (UN), *An Instructional Guide to Teaching about United Nations* (New York: UN Publication, 1993).
2. *Ibid.*
3. See Ruth Rocha and O. Roth, *Universal Declaration of Human Rights (UDHR)* (New York: UNI 1998).
4. *Ibid.*

Rights (UDHR) (New York: UNP,1998).
4. *Ibid.*
5. See the web *http//www.hri.ca.com*
6. See Ruth Rocha, *UDHR*, No.3
7. *Ibid.*
8. *Ibid.*
9. *Ibid.*
10. Cited in M.S. Swaminathan, "Food, Peace and Development", *The Hindu,* 29 November 2000.
11. William Korey, "NGOs: Fifty Years of Advocating Human Rights", Issues of Democracy, *USIA Electronic Journals*, Vol. No.3, October 1998, pp. 42–52.
12. *Ibid.*
13. See *UDHR*, No.2.
14. *Ibid.*
15. *Ibid.*
16. *Issues of Democracy*, No.12.
17. Cited from Website *http//www.hri.ca.com*
18. *Ibid.*
19. *Ibid.*
20. *The Pioneer* (New Delhi), 13 October 2000.
21. *Ibid.*
22. *Ibid.*
23. See Website, No.17.
24. *UN Information Kit, Decades for Eradicating Poverty 1999-2000* (NY: UNP, 1999), pp. 28–30.
25. See Intermediate School Kit on the United Nations (NY: UNP, 1995), pp. 31–32.
26. *Ibid.*
27. *Ibid.*
28. M. Sivaraman, "World March of Women", *People Democracy*, Vol. 24, No. 46, Nov. 12, 2000, p. 12.
29. *Ibid.*
30. *Ibid.*
31. *Ibid.*
32. See *Peace March* (Dharwad), Vol. 2, No. 7 July–August 1999. p. 5
33. *National Herald* (New Delhi), 13 October, 2000.
34. *The Pioneer* (New Delhi), 13 October 2000.
35. See *Intermediate School Kit*, No.25, p. 49.

Chapter - 5

Transforming Rural India

Introduction

The history of rural India dates back to the history of nation that originated in the form of well-developed peaceful society—the Harappan civilization—organized by Dravidians in the Indus Valley during the period of 6th millennium B.C. Dravidians settled in and around Baluchistan (Pakistan) and had knowledge about construction of break houses, domestication of cattle and cultivation of wheat.[1] Also, they had knowledge on copper that was turned out to be the primemover for exchange of goods among people in the later period modestly facilitating the economic transaction leading to value economy. However, the system of Harappan knowledge on development of society was diluted later due to the succession of foreigners— Aryans, Greeks, Persians, Mughal, British, Portuguese and French. Various rulers of foreign dynasties such as the Shakas, the Kushans, the Maurayas and Guptas further had influenced it.

At present India, with an area of 3.3 million sq km, is a country with probably the largest and most diverse mixture of races like Australoid, Mongoloid, Europoid, Caucasian and Negroid. Housing a variety of ethnic, linguistic and cultural groups, India stands unique in the history of humanity with the number of 1,027 million population of which more than 70 per cent of the people live in rural India speaking for about 17 major languages and 844 different dialects apart from number of other unclassified tribal languages.[2] In a report released in Population Day on 11 July 2003, it is stated that India shares 17 per cent of the world population, which crossed now 6 billion, 2.5 per cent in land and 23 per cent in growth. According to the report, the population growth in India is estimated to be 18 million, which is equal to that of Australian population. India thus produces one Australia every year. Whereas its per capita cropland is the lowest in the world.[3] Against this brief background, this chapter aims at providing new development agenda for transforming rural India in the twenty first century.

Conceptual Explanation

For development of a society, peace order is pertinent. A society without social harmony cannot develop. Even if it develops, it will not be permanent. Therefore, peace, as a dynamic incentive, plays a central role in development. A nation like India, having 700 million people living in 6,00,000 villages with different social, religious and communal groupings should necessarily establish peace order without which it cannot have last longing development.[4] As of the reason, social transformation can only take care of the development of India in general and rural India in particular.

Various methods can be adopted for getting people of India prepared for achieving the task of transforming rural India. In this context it may be stated that the 'India shining campaign' and 'feel good factor approach' of a National Democratic Alliance (NDA), which was defeated in 2004 and 2008 elections is a psychological one aimed at boosting up morale of the people for working towards the goal of developed India by 2020. Psychological approach may not help exclusively the suffering poor people for overcoming economic problems. Probably that was the reason why the NDA faced such a fate in the elections.

Secondly, knowledge economy—information based economy, is explained in this chapter with the intention of highlighting its use in transforming rural India. Rural India is not rural in the sense understood by many. Rather, it is an India with the power of knowledge, pertinent for present century. Further, it is an India with abundant human potential which can provide not only the leadership in knowledge sector but also in the political sector. Rural people can only provide good leadership for ruling the nation ably as it has staggering population strength around 700 million people. It should be mentioned here that the twenty-five European Union (EU) countries put together have only 445 million people and that rural population of India alone could surpass, therefore, it is more than fifty countries in the world including all European countries.[5] Apart from physical strength, rural India has lavish knowledge power unexploited, as noted above.

Traditional knowledge in many fields from astronomy to agriculture is appreciated but not applied for the benefit of rural people of India effectively. For instance, hundreds of years ago, India could generate the power of knowledge responsible for a cycle of discovery from the very school of Aryabhatta, who taught the entire world the method of counting by a great innovative invention of Zero. But, India lacked in utilizing it comparing to western counties, which had exploited the Indian knowledge for the benefits of their people and made out of it various fascinating technologies that were bought by India for a huge amount of money.[6] It is not that only India alone could not afford to explore its own traditional knowledge system for the benefits of its people it is the case with many African and Asian countries.

In the Agricultural sector, India stands first in the world since it has more than 50 per cent of its agricultural lands and a large number of farmers with potential knowledge on cultivation of various crops. In fact, India had taught the world as to how to cultivate most of the agricultural produces that are sent in the world market from different countries today. Knowledge among people, especially in cultivating the popular agricultural produces like pepper, chilly, plantation, sugarcane and cotton, is very great.[7] Such power of knowledge bestowed with rural people has to be ably utilized in order to take care for eliminating their poverty. India is the country today despite of all the advantages of having possessed pertinent knowledge, leads in the committee of nations with 220 million people living below poverty line (BPL).

India has missed to utilize the industrial age that ended in 1960 and information age between 1960s and 1990s. In fact, India has realized the information age acutely only when it entered into the process of globalization half-heartedly in 1991. In the same year, the knowledge age was dawned and witnessed a new plethora of international politics with the demise of Soviet Union, the fall of Berlin Wall, the fading of cold war and the new economic thrust for globalization through World Trade Organization (WTO), which emerged on 1 January 1995 after the Uruguay Round of GATT.[8] It should be noted here that due to the Structural Adjustment Programme (SAP) of the World Bank/IMF, India entered into the phases of both globalization (the corporate driven agenda for removing all barriers to profit) and localization (the people driven agenda for introducing ecological limits and social responsibility) without any serious homework. As a result balancing the economic activities in a new environment has delayed India to face the globalization process effectively. However, investment opportunities in India had been in increasing trend since 1991.

As a result, through 301 clauses of the US Trade Act many companies had entered into India.[9] For instance, Cargill—the largest grain trade and biggest seed company; Bechtel—the world largest construction company; General Electric—the popular power company; Dupont—the nylon plant and Enron—the gas and power corporation had already entered into India, despite massive protests launched against these transnational companies by people of India in various States.[10]

In the beginning, people were very critical about India's access to globalization. In the later stage, the opposition to this process was mellowed down due to the realization of the emerging new world. However, still the opposition against the issues relating to trade, agricultural produces, the regulation of WTO and the role of Multinational Corporations (MNCs) are continuing from certain quarters of the people. Despite, India goes ahead in implementing certain provisions of WTO by carefully protecting all products including the agricultural produces—from production to marketing, and accordingly generating support from many developing countries.[11] Brazil and China are working along with India to create conducive trade climate with proper security umbrella for developing countries. They have been trying to promote the views of poor farmers from Latin America, Africa and Asia. In the recently held Cancun Summit in 2003, developing countries views were further promoted and good response from developed countries are still awaited. While Indian economy shows the symptom of improvement after its entry into the globalizing process, the improvement of agro economy is yet to be seen.

Awakening rural poor with their rich, potentials are, therefore, important to withstand the on-going process of globalization.[12] It is also important to note about the ground reality of rural India today, which has been getting developed as per government plan from 1952 when the first ever community development movement was launched. In addition, in 1971 *'garibi hatao'* movement for eradicating poverty as a whole was launched by the then Prime Minister, Indira Gandhi. Unfortunately, they were not very successful. As a result, 320 million people live without basic amenities in India. Rural poverty remains the highest in Orissa, Bihar and Madhya Pradesh.[13] An action is needed, instead of criticizing the globalization process. In this context, 189 countries in the United Nations (UN) Millennium Summit also adopted a historic Millennium Declaration in September 2000, which specifically appealed to all the developing countries to transform their respective nation by way of eradicating poverty by 2015. India has adhered to the Millennium goal and since then it has been working accordingly.

Vision-2020

Transforming rual India needs a concerted plan. It is a nation building process, which involves in the development of people in various fields including politics, economics, science and technology, defence and international affairs. Therefore, it is viewed as a process of human resource development. So far as transforming rural Inida is concerned it is nothing but transforming India in general. Historically, India has had very good leaders with the vision of developing India. For instance, Mahatma Gandhi had vision for developing India based on his plan of 'Sarvodaya' through community development at village level.[14] In the globalizing world of today, a plan recognized to be a 'new sarvodaya' by many Gandhians for developing rural India in particular and India in general was proposed by not less than a person like the former President of India, Dr. A. P. J. Abdul Kalam. His message for developed India by 2020 is a new way for transforming India. It was considered by the government and accordingly the decision making process was initiated to fulfil the objectives.

All political parties, although they may differ in approaches, have approved of the vision 2020. As a result a parliamentary committee was formed up and it had approved a vision document with certain regulation to attain the status of developed India by 2020.[15] Freedom, Democracy and Development of people are given with priority in this document for overall economic prosperity irrespective of any identity. The document covers agriculture, power, information and communication technology, industrial and education sectors, space, nuclear, defence technologies, chemical, pharmaceutical, infrastructural industries and oil exploration. The sector-wise mission on realizing the vision is initiated on:[16]

- *Networking of Rivers* for eliminating the periodical problems of droughts and floods;
- *Quality Power* aiming at providing uninterrupted power by enhancing the output from one lakh megawatts to three lakh megawatts through sustainable energy resources like bio-mass, wind, solar energy apart from the power generated through hydel, thermal, and nuclear;

- *Providing Urban Amenities in Rural Areas*(PURA) through physical, electronic and knowledge connectivities, leading to self-sustained economic prosperity for groups of villages;
- *Information and Communication Technology* (ICT) by focussing on generating wealth of nation and by effective use of ICT in the areas of tele-medicine, tele-education, and e-governance;
- *Tourism* development by giving importance for inland water navigation, hotels, communication and tourist promotion; and
- *Enriching Village Life* by giving importance to children education and rights for growth of the society, avoiding gambling and liquor, becoming role models to children, cultivating learning, knowledge enrichment and success, protecting forest and preventing pollution and planting five trees or sapling at least.

Achieving 'PURA'

Apart from general vision with mission for developed India by 2020, a separate treatment for rural development is also advocated in the vision document specifically covering certain important areas for developing villages in areas like health care, education, networking of rivers, knowledge connectivity and transportation facilities by connecting villages to the mainstream of the cities.[17] As noted above, India is the country having maximum number of villages in the world. According to statistics, there are more than 6,00,000 villages in India. The proposal—PURA (Providing Urban Amenities in Villages) needs the government to concentrate on developing villages similar to that of urban areas of India. According to it, whatever facilities bequeathed in the urban areas should also be provided in the villages. Such development would arrest the exodus of villagers to the urban areas making the urban management easy.

The government should plan according to PURA and create more jobs for rural youths in the rural settings and urban mobility towards villages. In this connection, 30 million jobs are planned to be created in addition to 20 million through special programmes to be launched by both the centre and States and 8 per cent growth target has been set by Planning Commission. Thus, 10 million jobs per year to be created for taking care of the unemployed and underemployed people. The growth and development path, which is in different setting now due to globalization, is also planned to be in a new environment wherein the cost cutting and competitiveness hold the key to success.[18] Also, there have been diferent approaches to growth — export growth, labour intensive growth and focus on service sector which is now leading. The private sectors are chosen as engines of growth by the government. However, it is important to note that the private sectors will concentrate only on profits and exports facing the competition rather than generating more jobs for unemployed people.

Moreover, the government had set up a task force on job creation so as to find out various new means in this direction. It should also be mentioned that since the agri, plantation and manufacturing sectors are looking for more machines in respective field, it is not likely that the government can generate 30 million jobs. So far as the industries are concerned they want the government do away from the labour law which are not, according to them, suit the existing globalized trend especially considering on competition.[19] As a matter of fact reforms and growth have become unfortunately the antithesis of labour and employments in the era of liberalization and Gobalization.

Thus, growth with employment generation seems to be very tuff, which may go against the interests of government for producing 10 million jobs a year. Moreover, the trend is not encouraging as the public sectors are freezing employment and wages. The task force should, therefore, make an arrangment for creating more jobs even in the public sectors by wooing the private sectors invest in new and innovative areas so as to generate more jobs.[20]

In the food sector, India is planning to feed the entire poulation with suffficient foodstuff thereby making India hunger free. For attaining the goal, the government is planning to adopt the following measures:[21] taking care of the pregnant and nursing mothers, infants and pre-school children, youth, adult, old and infirm persons in the rural India in particular; developing community food Banks; promoting National Food Guarantee Scheme(NFGS); sustaining and strengthening agricultural progress and management of changes especially in reference to technology, ecology and trade; implementing Grain Bank Scheme (GBS) in tribal areas and Sampoorna Gramin Rozgar Yojana—food for work.

The recent initiatives in the power and transportation sectors, although it has certain drawbacks, is a welcome one. It should be noted that the government of India is planning to develop more power by exploring the means for involving the private sectors in the field of power production as well as transportation. Privatization in these areas are needed, but they have to be ably made to fall in line with government of India's regulation for the advantage of people. It is to be noted that the laying of four lane roads is very much in support of PURA.[22] If facilities that are available in urban India are provided in rural areas, people will enjoy freedom of exercising their duty in developing their areas by not thinking of coming out of their places for just pulling on their life.

Therefore, more employments should be created for rural youths who constitute nearly half of the population of India. If the rural youths are empowered, rural India will be more than urban India and the urban India will be atracted towards rural India. As of now, most of the educated people settling with jobs in urban India never even visit their native places in the rural settings. According to NCERT reports, nearly eighty per cent of the educated masses are from rural areas. But they are all alienated from the rural settings depriving the villages from enjoying the fruits of their labours.[23] This has been the situation for the last fifty seven years now. It is also reported that most of the fertile lands are not cultivated due to lack of farmers in the villages.

For the reasons that create an artificial attraction for the city life what one calls as 'urban maya', the rural people are heading towards cities by seeking and finally settling down with some 'third rate' jobs unmindful of their lands, aged parents and close relatives. Due to this, interests of youths for cultivating their lands are vanishing away overall. This trend is existing all over India, from south to north and from east to west. How to make the younger generation to get involved, with dignity in the field of agriculture?, how to make the urban settled educated masses to get access to their own villages?, how to make the unemployed youths of rual as well as urban areas to get involved in the nation building process?, how to fuse all sections of people for achieving the task of transforming rural India?, how to set action plan for developing rural India?, and how to establish knowledge links for overall growth aiming at achieving developed India by 2020? These are some of the questions bothering the minds of many people concerned about transforming rural India today.

Knowledge Revolution in Rural India

To give shape to the vision of converting India into a knowledge superpower, initiatives were taken by the Union Cabinet from 2003 and a panel of experts were appointed for directing all the ministries, related administrators to work for the objective. According to the panel members the proposed plan for making India a knowledge superpower will include the networking of important areas such as education, health, information technology (IT), bio-technology and financial services. To this effect, the Planning Commission has unveiled a report on India Vision-2020 on 24 January 2003.[24] According to it, the Government of India plans to provide 100 per cent elementary education to rural people apart from eliminating poverty and unemployment. It also aims at increasing the per capita income of the rural people so as to attain a GDP growth of 9 per cent per annum by 2020. The government consequently envisions that the entire population of 1.35 billion will be better fed, dressed and housed, healthier, more edeucated and longer living than any generation in the history of India.

More interestingly, it also envisions that the employment in this sector would fall from 56 to 40 per cent in the coming years and, therefore, it will be managed by creating more jobs in the unorganized labour sectors mostly from small and medium scale industries, transport, agriculture, agro-forestry, fisheries, tourism, IT education and health.[25] The Planning Commission also recommends that the Government of India should make the rights for the job as constitutional one and manage to control the flow of rural population to urban areas. It is expected that the urban population would rise from 25.5 per cent to 40 per cent in the coming years.[26] Providing urban amenities in the rural areas in related fields of trade, technology and investment can help the rural masses to settle down in their respective villages.

Therefore, value added information—referred as knowledge, has to reach the rural people. All the instruments required have to be transmitted and properly installed in places from where people can have access to vital information on various fields like health, education, cultivation, fishing, climate and employment. If there is any constraint faced in the knowledge network, relevant actions to overcome such constraint has to be immediately initiated.[27] Through demand driven information, knowledge centres have to be built by training the local people to operate the centres and own the same in course of time. For, 'antyodaya model' has to be adopted which will take care of the deprived people, especially the women and children, unable and old people in their respective areas.

For effective functioning of these knowledge centres 'malady remedy' analysis should be adopted so as to meet out the requirements with available technologies. For instance, wired and wireless technologies could be used where telephone connections are not adequate.[28] Effective usages of technology can thus help the rural masses by empowering them in the information field. Such initiatives, the Information and Communication Technology (ICT) can help establish the following facilities for the purpose of empowering people and, therefore, for transforming rural India as a whole with the sole aim of eradicating poverty by providing employment to all: [29]

- *Farm Net* for agricultural workers;
- *Telecentres* for economic empowerment of women;
- *Rural Multipurpose Community Telecentres* for libraries and online facilities;
- *Mahila Web* for information sharing about the problems of women and gender;
- *Rural e-commerce portal* for homemade rural products especially made by women;
- *Rural e- Banks* for facilitating the deserving community in the local areas;
- *Rural Market Watch* for price information service;
- *Web services centres* for slum children;
- *Street Children Telecentres* for developing IT skills;
- *Centres for knowledge sharing* on important events of rural India among rural people;
- *Centres for renewable energy*, agro-industry, vegetable and fruit research;
- *Virtual Marketplaces* for underprivileged artisans in the rural areas;
- *Multipurpose Community Telecentres* in farming and fishing villages of rural areas;
- *GrameenPhone Centres* connecting nearby urban centrees;
- *E-Health Information Centres* for all the people living in and around rural areas;
- *Communication Boat Projects* to bring IT tools via boats to rural areas;

- *Project Cybercare* for providing Internet access and educational resources to orphanages;
- *E-centres* for sharing knowledge among rural people on sustainable natural resource management;
- *Rural Studios* for developing reusable software components and services for the rural development sector; and
- *E-governance Grid val* a network of information kiosks providing sales tax forms, income certificates, domicile certificates, caste certificates, ration card forms, driving licence, company registration, *khasra*-land records, landholder's passbook of land rights and loans, rural language e-mail, commodity/mandi marketing information system, public grievance redressal, forms of various government schemes, below poverty line family list, employment and matrimonial news, rural news papers, e-advise for conflict resolution including in the family economy management, and free eeducation for rural children.

For instance, M.S. Swaminathan Research Foundation has been doing the desirable jobs by setting up information villages in Tamilnadu and Pondicherry. The project established by the foundation in Pondicherry has won the Stockholm Challenge Award under the Global Village category 2001.[30] It plays an important role in building a knowledge based electronic rural society connecting villages through a hybrid wired and wireless network—PCs, telephones, VHF duplex radio devices, e-mail and dial-up telephone lines, which facilitate both voice and data transfer enabling the villagers to get vital information for their day-to-day life. It accentuates an integrated pro-poor, pro-women, pro-nature orientation to development, helps the community own the technological tools and encourages collective action involving local volunteers to gather information, feed it into an internet for providing access to different villages.[31]

Thus, the project demonstrates in this part of the country

that empowering people by providing access to relevant information can make a difference in the life of the rural poor and that the ICT can play a crucial role apart from disseminating vital information on prices of agricultural inputs such as seeds, fertilizers, pesticides; outputs—rice, vegetables, market; entitlement to the large number of schemes of the central and State governments; health care information relating to the availability of doctors, paramedics in nearby hospitals, women's diseases, cattle diseases; transport relating to road conditions and cancellation of bus trips and weather condition for sowing as well as fishing.[32] Hence, powering rural people with knowledge will help transform the rural India.

Conclusion with Suggestions

Since 1952, India has been striving to transfer rural India with the support of many institutions, individuals and organizations. At present, there are a number of schemes embarked on for this purpose in accordance with UN millennium goal approved by 189 countries, including India in 2000. India, therefore, should rejuvenate itself, without merely feeling proud of participating in the globlization process or achievement in the field of ICT. It has to have 'people centric' plan instead of 'ICT centric'.[33]

Harnessing advantages from emerging S&T areas, therefore, need a long sighted plans with instant use for the 'common man'. ICT can only play as a launchpad not a benevolent. It should be made as people friendly. Pompous propoganda about the advantages of the computers will not help the people. People should buy the computers according to their requirements not for keeping these for status. Such attitude will neither help the buyers nor the sellers in the long run. The utility related information according to the life style of the owners or prospering new customers of PC should, therefore, reach before the machine. It happened in China, a country which had only less than two computer per thousand in 1998 while comparing to India which had more than three computers in the same year.

Today, it has almost equalised with India in promotion of computers. In addition, the percentage of utility of the existing computers in India is incredibly minimum. It demonstrates the weakness of users who do not utilize it for their maximum advantage.

Hence, mere promotion of computers alone will not make 'India shine' or 'feel good' in general. That too in the rural areas, it will not help improve the situation. Promotion of community radios, TVs and health centres, for instance, in India are not serving the purpose. Rather, they are all playing as the sources of social conflicts in various rural pockets. Also, the scientific devices in general and computers in particular will not automatically generate employments and help eradicate poverty among the most deserving 220 million people living below poverty line. As of these reasons, providing people with the technological access on vital information for building a cohesive knowledge society should be on the ground reality of the "utility based demand-oriented-economy" of the rural people not of the market oriented one.

Therefore, the globalization process set on the fast track economy through structural adjustment scheme has to be utilized efficiently first by serving the poor people of India without bothering too much for idealistic developments.[34] Aiming to make India a hunger free nation and to eradicate poverty as a whole by 2015 are the most important agenda for development in this respect. As a matter of fact, synergy of science and technology transfers are vital elements for achieving this goal with priority based approaches. India, being a predominantly agricultural country, where more than 625 million farmers live in, should allocate extra attention, money and technological investments by establishing added infrastructural facilities in this basic field.

The first green revolution has placed India in the phase of self-sufficiency in production of foodgrains. Indian farmers could achieve this with the able leadership and counselling by efficient scientists. The second phase of revolution should be launched with revitalized vigour and take care of the sprawling Indian GDP. The other priority area in which the government should concentrate now is on basic education and health with the commitment of accomplishing 100 per cent literacy and health care facilities in rural India. In addition, the government should plan for such an education, which would provide employment and help people in the long run to achieve productivity-oriented literacy and to participate in the higher education leading to research in specialized areas.

To this effect, immediate attention has to be drawn for increasing the percentage of higher education from 6 per cent to 30 per cent by empowering the existing universities and by establishing new universities in the coming years. Both the agricultural and educational fields can transform rural India more efficiently than any other fields. Such transformation will pave the way for a developed India in the future. Therefore, the new secular government led by Congress-I has to work not only for accelerating employment, growth and investment but also for providing social harmony, peace and 'purposeful knowledge' infrastructure. Such works of the government with vision would transform the rural India and promote the welfare of the farmers, farm labourers, youths, women and weaker sections.

NOTES

1. See, Moorthy P., "Indus Valley to Silicon Valley: A Study on Knowledge Economy and Global Peace" *Peace March* (Dharward), Vol. 1, No. 5, Oct–Dec. 2002, pp. 24–32
2. See the *Report of National Commission on Population* cited in *The Hindu* (Chennai), 12 July 2003
3. *Ibid.*
4. Moorthy P., "*Indus Valley to Silicon Valley*", No.1.
5. See *www.EMERGIC.org.com*
6. *Ibid.*
7. Moorthy P., "*Indus Valley to Silicon Valley*", No.1.
8. See for a good analysis on globalization Breton Gilles and Michel Lambert (ed.) *Universities and Globalization: Private Linkages* (Paris: UNESCO Publishing, 2003).

9. *The Hindu*, 25 June 2003, also Prabir Purkayastha, 'Ancient Civilizations and the Aryan race', *People Democracy* (New Delhi), October 15 2000, p. 5
10. *Ibid.*
11. *The Hindu*, 28 January 2003.
12. *Ibid.*
13. *Ibid.*, See for a successful case study, *Panchayati Raj and the Decentralization of Development Planning in West Bengal*: A Case *Study*. Neil Webster, CDR Project Paper No.7, Center for Development Research, Copenhagen 1990.
14. See A.P.J. Abdul Kalam, Y.S. Rajan, *India 2020: A Vision for the New Millennium*(New Delhi: Viking Press, 1998).
15. *Ibid.*
16. *Ibid.*
17. *Ibid.*, See also Robert Chambers. "The Origins and Practice of Participatory Rural Appraisal", *World Development* (New York), Vol. 22, No. 7, July 1994, pp. 234–42.
18. *United Nations (UN) Weekly* (New Delhi), No. 2, Vol. 1, 2003, p. 6.
19. *Ibid.*
20. See *Indian Express*(Chennai), 6. June 2003.
21. See the *Report of National Commission on Population,* No.2.
22. *Ibid.*
23. *The Hindu*,18 January 2003; see also Rural Transport in Developing Countries, Barwell, I.; Edmonds G. A.; Howe, J. D. G. F.; and de Veen, J., *Intermediate Technology Publications*, London, 1985 presents the findings of these first reasearch efforts to define the nature of rural people's transport needs and the various constraints which these have to be satisfied.
24. *The Hindu*, 25 January 2003, For good reading in this aspect See, Gary Hammel, *Leading the Revolution* (New York: Harvard Business School Press, 2000).
25. See the *Report of National Commision on Population*, No.2
26. *Ibid.*
27. See M.S. Swaminathan, 'Fighting Hunger: Know 'How' to "Do how", *The Hindu* (Chennai), 23, June 2002.
28. *Ibid.*
29. *www.EMERGIC. org.com* No.5; For Guidelines for rural centre planning, See the United Nations, *Economic and Social Commission for Asia and the Pacific* (New York:UN Press, 1979).
30. M.S. Swaminathan, *'Fighting Hunger'*, No. 27.

31. *Ibid*., for good planning for rural development, See G. Edmonds, C. Donnges and N. Palarca, *Guidelines on Integrated Rural Accessibility Planning* (Manila: ILO/DILG Press, 1994).
32. http://*www.International/ Knowledge Management News Letter. com*
33. See Brian K. Williams, Stacey C. Sawyer, and Sarah E. Hutchinson (edit.), *Using Information Technology: A Practical Introduction to Computers and Communications* (Boston: McGraw Hill, 1999).
34. See for a good reading in this respect, Anisur Rahman, *People's Self-Development : Perspectives on Participatory Action Research*, (London: ZED Books, 1993).

Chapter - 6

Disaster Management : The Case of 'Tsunami'

"One thing I have learned in a long life:
all our science measured against reality is primitive and childlike—
and yet it is the most precious thing we have"

—Albert Einstein

Introduction

From the dawn of history, humanity has been suffering devastating losses from the natural disaster like earthquake, volcano, tornado, hurricane, tsunami, etc. As natural disaster occurs at any time without warning, it is considered more dangerous than the man-made weapons of mass destruction. Such phenomenal activities of nature have been occurring for billions of years. According to scientists, the history of natural disaster dates back to the history of the Earth.[1] However, only after the origin of human life on Earth galvanized by Moon, these natural activities have come under scrutiny. Even after having thousands of years of experiences on these phenomenal occurrences of nature from the Indus Valley civilization to the 'Silicon Valley Civilization', —Information Technology (IT) leading to the establishment of Knowledge Society—perfect understanding as to what causes these disasters and how to escape from them is not achieved. Against this backdrop, this chapter aims at exploring the means for managing natural disaster in general and tsunami in particular by analyzing issues pertinent for establishing perfect understanding with nature.

Understanding the Origin of Disaster

More than 15 billion years ago, matters were tightly clumped together. Mass and energy were found only after the 'big bang phenomenon', that created stars, galaxies, cluster of galaxies, super clusters, interstellar dust, planets, meteorites, and comets. According to the scientists, they are all self-gravitative mass accumulations.[2] Although the occurrence of big bang was so complex in nature to understand, it is generally agreed that it had occurred due to the nebula gases and their action and reaction phenomenon mixing with clumped matter. Nebula is an enormous cloud of interstellar gas, which is made of atoms and tiny particles. The solar system, being a leader in the process, had birth from the revolving masses of incandescent gases. The condensation of the solar nebula to form the Sun occurred approximately 4.5 to 4.6 billion years ago by violent mix-up of matter and anti-matter creating repulsive nuclear forces that explosively blew this concentrated mass apart.[3] The Sun is a huge glowing ball of gases made of 90 per cent hydrogen atoms, about nine per cent helium atoms and one per cent other elements, such as oxygen and nitrogen.

In this great family of the solar system, the accumulative formation of Earth and other planets from planetesimals—meteorites, asteroids and comets—took place concurrently. It should be noted here that the origin of the solar system and its family is determined through the investigation of meteorites and lunar samples. Earth is roughly a ball like in shape. Seventy one per cent of the earth is covered by water and twenty nine per cent by the land. It is made up of several layers, which can be divided into three main layers—crust, mantle and the central core. The upper most crust varies in thickness from about eight kilometres under the oceans to about forty kilometres under the continents. The crust is mainly composed of silica, which is divided into layers—the upper layer consisting of silica-magnesium, and the heavier-lower sial with silica-aluminium. Mantle is the next layer below the crust made of solid rock largely containing magnesium. The innermost core is made of two layers consisting of iron and nickel alloy under pressure. It is also surrounded by thick liquid outer core composed mainly of nickel and iron and also silicon and sulfur.[4]

It is important to understand the sulfur, a deeply seated substance in the interior of the Earth, which is spilled out by volcanic eruption. Earlier days, the volcanic deposit of sulfur were understood as brimstone that had played central role for the expansion of scientific knowledge contributing various scientific inventions in course of time. For instance, the importance of sulfur can be understood through the definition of the concepts, known as sulfate reduction and sulfuretum. Sulfate reduction is the metabolic process that converts sulfate to sulfide, oxidizing organic material in the process and sulfuretum is an environment in which the various metabolic transformation of the sulfur cycle takes place. Thus, it had played a great role, as scientists note, in the evolution of organic life and the environment accordingly.[5] The Romans had used volcanic deposit what they called as Pozzolana for construction work in the early period of 10 AD and the deposit—Colsseum, found in the Mediterranean Island of Thera during the period of 70 AD, was used for the construction of the Suez Canal in the 19th century. The great volcanic activities of the Earth are also responsible for the formation of gold, one of the most precious element of the Earth, which has been playing a predominant role in the human created value economy of the present world.

The negative side of the volcanic activities was witnessed by the people of the world for the first time in 1702 when it had erupted on the Mount Pelee in the Caribbean Isand of Martinique, killing 28,000 inhabitants. It is important to note here that most of the Caribbean countries are not only vulnerable for natural onslaughts but also for the human-made poverty. In 1985, volcanoes have killed more than 25,000 people in Colombia. It is reported that the volcanoes have killed totally 2,60,000 lives since 1700.[6] Scientists, studying on volcanic activities, note that the countries not experienced the volcanic eruption in the past will face this phenomenal occurrence of nature in the future due to the violent tectonic activities making unprecedented combination of continental rift.

The Earthquake

Earthquake is a sudden and rapid shaking of the Earth caused by the breaking and shifting of rock beneath the Earth's surface that sometimes trigger landslides, avalanches, flash floods, fires, and huge destructive ocean waves—named in Japanese language as 'tsunami.' Since it occurs without any warning due to various phenomenal forces operating underneath earth, as noted above, it creates sudden changes at the face of the Earth spilling out excessive power of energy. It also changes gradually the characteristics of the earth by mild way of expression of its lesser power of energy that does not disrupt the normal life setting of human beings as well as the existence of lives. Thousands of such earthquakes and volcanoes have occurred changing the very shape of the planet Earth by creating rivers, ravine, mountains etc. apart from contributing to the formation of climates.[7] It is to be noted that the two biggest earthquakes occurred in Huahsien, in 1556 killing 8,20,000 people and in Tang Shan, China in 1976 killing 2,40,000 people have played very important role in understanding about the impact of these natural occurrence, especially the earthquake. It is also worth noting here that because of its early experiences on earthquake and related seismic behaviour of Earth, China could contribute for the development of scientific knowledge apart from possessing various core elements of the Earth pertinent for further research.

In the ancient times, Greeks understood earthquake in mythological way. They believed that due to evil spirit the earthquakes occurred. The popular belief during that period was that the gods of Olympus had buried monstrous called Titans under the Phlegraen Fields after defeating them and the Titans' violent attempts to free themselves from the Earth had caused shaking of the earth with fiery outburst of volcanic eruptions. However, in the 5th century, Thales of Miletus (624-546 BC), noted to be the first philosopher and first scientist of the world, had initiated study on earth activities differing from the mythological understandings. However, he could not understand the earth as he was in the opinion that the Earth was seated on water.[8] Followed by him, Pythagoras of Samos (540–510 BC.) had believed that the fire was located in the centre of the Earth, which was responsible for the occurrence of earthquakes or volcanoes. The scientific tradition had continued with the array of scholars increasingly showing interests on these subjects of studies from the early period onwards. Some of the prominent thoughts of men on these phenomenons are noted below:[9]

- Anaxagoras of Clazomenae (500–428 BC) believed that air within earth was the creator of earthquake and volcanoes;
- Democritus of Abdera (400 BC), the founder of atomic theory and who noted that the trapped air into the earth was the possible agent for volcanoes;
- Aristotle (384-322 BC) believed that all matters were mixture or combination of five elements—earth, water, air, fire and celestial bodies like stars, sun, etc.;
- Thucydides, the great historian staying in Sicily, had reported the earliest historic eruption of volcanoes during 424–403 BC and who believed that bad spirit was the cause for earthquake;
- Saint Augustine (354-430 AD) had banned the entire spectrum of the natural sciences that were developed in antiquity propagating that "heavenly and earthly bodies were created by the goodness of the creator, the one true God";
- Saint Brendan (484-574 AD), a navigator who was in search of Paradise thinking that North Atlantic region would have such place had encountered ruff sea during his travel and shown interest on understanding the earthly events in the latter period of his life;

- Thomas Hobbes (1558–1679), the philosopher and atheist, who had ridiculed the theological cosmography of the under world stated water and air inside earth were responsible for earthquake.;
- Isaac Newton (1642–1727) had concluded in his study that the "earth by heat becomes fire and by cold returns into earth". His great discovery on gravitational energy was published in 1887 that helped advance the study relating to earthquake;
- Robert Boyle, Robert Hooke, and Richard Lower had worked on sulfur and regarded it as spiritus nitro-aereus (oxygen). Boyle work was continued by the French chemist, Antoine Lavoisier (1743-1794);
- Immanuel Kant (1724-1804) had published his work on nebular hypothesis that made a revolutionary changes in understanding about the solar system and its family including the earth and its seismic behaviour,
- Williams Hopkins, the English geophysicist, had worked on thermodynamics—the study of the fundamental laws of energy and heat that had considerable lead in the study of earth science during 18th century;
- Author Holmes, studying about the origin of volcanoes and magmas, discovered in 1904 that the radioactive decay of certain chemical elements with the earth was responsible for providing the heat source to drive the convection currents.

The above evolution of thoughts on Universe had contributed for the progressive expansion of knowledge on the Earth and its phenomenal activities in the twentieth century. As a result, the ancient fire that came out the earth and its chemical components were identified and put in proper use. For instance, the ancient men of China had learned to use such fire 60,000 years ago for making pots. A similar kind of discovery in Kenya in 1993 had proved that people living in Chesowanja had knowledge of fire and its usage million and half years ago. Thus, people have been advancing in understanding the earthly events and their action and reaction phenomenon quite efficiently from ancient time onwards.

According to the recent studies, continental African plates, as scientists note, pushes inexorably northward at a rate of about 1 centimetre (0.4 inch) per year, weakening the floor of the Mediterranean Sea gradually deforming it and contributing for earthquake. Scientists, working on relatively new landmass on Earth, could also understand these phenomenal activities of nature. It is reported that the landmass of North America, specifically Canada, is new one as its ice sheet of several kilometres thick covering most of Canada was melted and finally disappeared over Hudson's Bay only for about 6,000 years ago due to the sea level that rose by more than 100 metres.[10] Scientists, researching on Asian plates, note that due to the changing seismic activism all over the Earth, earthquake may occur in different places of Asian countries in the future.

India has experienced a major earthquake in Bhuj in January 2004. According to the latest report, one or more massive earthquakes may occur in the Himalayan region, wherein 50 million people are living. For about a century, India had not experienced earthquakes in this part of the country, as it was only in 1800s it had such calamity there. Scientist, analyzing the Sumatra earthquake that triggered the tsunami in the Indian Ocean on 26 December 2004, notes that similar earthquakes will hit the Indian Ocean in the future. In fact, on 15 March 2005, Indonesia was attacked by one more earthquake occurred 34 kilometres beneath the seabed. However, it did not trigger tsunami.[11] It is reported that 56 km stretch of the undersea Sunda trench next to the 1192 km long zone that created tsunami on December 26 and the city, Band Ache that is under reconstruction after severe destruction by tsunami, are considered more vulnerable for earthquakes in the coming years.

Earthquakes with greater magnitude had occurred in the same parts of Indonesia creating dangerous tsunami in 1883 and in 1861. Therefore, in the recently held conference among

Indian Ocean countries in Paris, all the countries along with the UN experts have agreed that since Indian Ocean region is becoming more and more earthquake active, viable early warning system should be installed as early as possible. For that purpose, works to establish the network of tidal gauges and seabed sensors by pooling varieties of technologies available with different member countries are initiated. Japan and the US are requested to help this effort especially by providing effective information on seismic activity of the Indian Ocean.[12]

'Tsunami' and the Indian Experiences

Tsunami—meaning 'harbuor wave' in Japanese language — is caused by sudden earthquake or underwater landslides. Tsunami flows towards the coastline rising to several feet and causes great loss of life and property. It can raise waves ranging from 10 feet to 100 feet high depending upon the magnitude with which it is generated by the forces of earthquake-induced movement of the ocean floor, landslides, volcanic eruptions and even by the fall of meteorites from the space. It also attacks farther inlands than the immediate coast by travelling through open canals and rivers that are connected with seas. It occurs in any season of the year, at any time, day or night, travelling at the speed of 450 to 600 miles per hour towards coastline.[13] As the waves approach the coastline, it can sometimes cause huge flood, contaminate drinking water by entering into the well and destroying the drinking water pipelines, make fires by collapsing the gas lines and petrol tanks, and hit the vital community infrastructure like Hospitals, Radio, Television stations, Schools and Colleges.

It is stated that a strong earthquake lasting for about twenty seconds or more near the coastline can also generate tsunami. Japan was attacked by tsunami much earlier than any other countries in the world. Followed by Japan many countries had fallen victims to this killer waves. Countries like Kenya and the US had registered the loss of life and property due to tsunami in the recent past. In fact, it hit Hawaii—the US—in 1994 killing more than 350 people and caused huge loss of property.[14] Since then, the US has been campaigning for establishing early warning system by pooling all the technologies that are available with different countries of the world. Accordingly, it has been formulating various measures for feasible implementation of an effective system in this respect, as it is the only power, which has demonstrative skill in implementation of various technologies starting from remote-sensing satellites to information and communication (ICT) related hand held cell phones of today.

On 26 December 2004, India has experienced such natural onslaught that has killed thousands of people apart from causing huge damage to the property and life settings of the poor people mostly fishing community. Although it did not suffer as much as Indonesia or Sri Lanka, the destruction was relatively more in Andaman and Nicobar Islands, Nagapattinam, Cuddalore and Kanya Kumari in Tamil Nadu. Andhra Pradesh, Kerala and Pondicherry were also considerably affected in lesser scale while comparing to Andaman and Tamil Nadu. Andaman and Nicobar Islands have experienced the geological changes due to earthquake.[15] It is reported that certain islands far away from each other have come closer after tsunami. Because of its unprecedented magnitude apart from killing more than 3 lakhs people of Indian Ocean community—the biggest tsunami of all the time in the human history, it had drawn the attention of the entire world community and made them generously extend helping hands to the affected nations.

Thousands of individuals, NGOs, army personnel, doctors, students and teachers have come forward to help tsunami-hit people of the Indian Ocean community. It is reported that 3.5 lakh people including a sizable number of foreigners in Tamilnadu and 48,000 people in Andaman are at work in the relief and reconstruction work even today especially involving themselves for supplying of regular food, health and sanitation facilities and house construction. However, it is reported that the rehabilitation work is not proceeding the way it should be due to various internal politics in India. As of the reasons, fishing communities have been agitating in different places. Despite, the political parties are not in unanimity of mind that is needed to help people in this crisis, which is viewed by the world community as the greatest opportunity to serve the humankind by overcoming political differences.[16]

The political situation in Tamil Nadu is worst, as ADMK and DMK have been in political tug of wars since the beginning of the relief work. The Central Government is also not showing interest to avoid such conflict with the tsunami-hit states, especially with Tamil Nadu because of the combination of political alliances. In 2005 the fishermen of Thevanampattinam and Parangipettai in Tamil Nadu have decided not to accept the financial help of the government, which is indifferent, according to them, in this serious crisis faced by the fishing community. Moreover, it is stated by them that the financial help extended to them is not fair enough. As of the reason, they have opposed specifically the decision of government for opening a joint Bank accounts in the name of the beneficiary and Joint Director of the Fisheries Department for depositing the relief money. In addition, they alleged that the government officials have undermined the extent of damage and sanctioned rupees only 40,000 for a fibre-reinforced boat that would require rupees one lakh.[17] In the case of Thevanampattinam, the fishermen alleged that the officials have fixed the compensation package without even visiting the village. It should be noted here that the relief works undertaken by Bollywood actor Vivek Oberoi in Thevanampattinam are appreciable and encouraging to the tsunami hit people that have helped them gain material as well as morale benefits. Since the allotted amount of rupees 32,000 for repairing catamaran is not reached on time, the fishermen of Cuddalore and nearby places have launched a public demonstration to highlight these basic issues.

In the case of Pondicherry, relief works are completed almost in all places like Karaikal, Murthikuppam, Akkarampettai and Chinnakalapet. Nevertheless, it is reported in Podicherry region, except at Murthikuppam, land identification has reached a roadblock with the people opposing relocation of fishermen anywhere near their hamlets. However, the non-governmental organization, SOS Children's Village was handed over nine acres of land by the Governor of Pondicherry recently for construction of 225 houses in Murthikuppam. Another 200 houses are planned for Akkarampettai in the months to come by the same NGO. It is also reported that the land allotment issues have created some discomfort among different communities in certain pockets of Pondicherry delaying both the relief as well as construction works apart from disturbing the social harmony. Although the present political scenario is not very conducive due to various issues cropped up within ruling as well as opposition parties, the reconstruction work may continue unaffected.

Meanwhile the damages and needs assessment report of the joint study of the World Bank, the Asian Development Bank (ADB) and the United Nations note that the relief and reconstruction works in the four mainland tsunami-affected States and Union territories are expected to reassess the situation especially relating to the estimated cost of relief and construction works. According to it, Tamil Nadu is the worst affected State, which needs 868 million dollars followed by Kerala (158 million), Pondicherry (114 million) and Andhra Pradesh (73 million). The overall damages to assets have been put at about 575 million dollars while the productivity losses have been placed at about 450 million. Reconstruction work for housing and fisheries are estimated to be 490 and 285 million respectively by this Report. Also, the Joint Assessment Team visited Tamil Nadu, Kerala, Andhra Pradesh and Pondicherry from 1 to 15 February, 2005 have studied the feasibility of rebuilding infrastructure, rehabilitation of livelihoods and develop disaster prevention and management systems for the future in these States. In total, as the report pointed out, India would need 1.2 billion for both relief and reconstruction work.[18]

Disaster Management

Tsunami occurred on 26 December, 2004 in Indian Ocean area and is recorded as one of the most destructive natural disasters in human history that has highlighted the importance of establishing effective disaster management system by utilizing science and technology of the present century cutting across the political and cultural differences that are 'man-made disasters' in the world. It also highlighted the vulnerability of the poor people especially living near seashore areas. It should be noted here that more number of poor people were victim and their properties were lost due to tsunami in the world. Moreover, it has highlighted the importance of understanding its hazardous nature when it occurs in thickly populated areas like India and accordingly considering the important issues with regard to the reconstruction and development strategy for disaster management based on participatory, equitable, flexible, decentralized and transparent approach.[19] It should be noted that more than 13 per cent of the world cyclone is occurring in the seas around India.

According to the UN report, better management of the coastal environment and reinforced risk reduction should be, therefore, seen as part of the overall social and economic strategy by considering the reconstruction work and new infrastructure development as social investments for which appropriate coastal regulation and risk management are necessary preconditions. Thus, the disaster management work has to be initiated independently getting into action immediately after the natural attack by motivating for increased participation of the local communities in the respective tsunami hit places.[20] Many experts on disaster managements have appreciated the UN initiative and requested it for exploring ways for lessening the impact of tsunami based on natural means rather than relying on artificial construction of concrete walls on the coastal lines. It is to be noted that awareness building among people is an important tenet for reducing the damages to the property and for saving the life of the people from the killer waves. Such activities would also help people from venturing into sea unmindful of the dangerous nature of tsunami.

For awareness activities, young people should be trained and given with needed assistance by setting up of trained search and rescue teams in districts and taluk levels. It is important that these groups of people should be given with all scientific devices like computers with internet facilities, cellophones and all other important equipments for tracking information and flashing the same to the people of affected areas. They should evaluate plans on regular basis based on the experiences gained through technological developments periodically and such advancement should be transmitted to the team of volunteers appointed in the local places joining with the elderly people of villages or village heads.[21] To sustain the development with regard to the disaster management, natural barriers like mangroves and coral reefs should be cultivated in the seashore areas and in the sea respectively.

It should be mentioned here that these natural barriers were destroyed by the recent tsunami largely in the Indian Ocean areas. The coral reef to be developed by natural process would take considerable period. It plays an important role for providing friendly life settings for fishes, tortoise and other living beings apart from providing balanced ecosystem in the coastline of the Indian Ocean.[22] As far as the mangroves are concerned, they can play an immediate role in preventing tsunami from entering into human settlement areas. Because of mangroves, it is reported that the nuclear plant areas of Kalpakkam was not attacked. In the east coast areas of the Indian Ocean, a large number of mangroves were destroyed due to tsunami. More than anything else, it is necessary to develop greater international cooperation and coordination for establishing effective early warning systems by integrating various technologies, especially the defence technology which have much relevance for developing useful disaster warning system. [23]

Disaster Warning System

Early warning system is increasingly being realised by the world nations for successful establishment of a communication network to predict and warn the disaster prone areas of the world much earlier than the occurrence of natural disasters. For such early warning communication network, primarily 'global seismograph network' is necessary to study the pressure wave of earth and their travel through earth's crust. Such technical expertise has been available in the world from the late 1959, when the US developed technological means to distinguish between large nuclear explosions underneath earth and the natural earthquake.[24] Today, its Geological Survey, funded by the Defence Department, has developed a worldwide network consisting of 'seismic listening stations' in over sixty countries to study the earthquakes and to monitor underground nuclear tests.

These installations are connected with the Vela satellite in the space located 70,000 miles away from the earth for establishing effective flash of communication to all the nations connected in this early warning network. The Vela satellite, launched in 1970, is now equipped with new detection sensors. For strengthening the efficacy of the network, the US has thousands of radar systems placed in different countries stretching from Alaska through Canada and Greenland into Iceland and Europe, Norway, Turkey, France, Spain, Japan, Australia and Philippines. As counter measure to the US, Russia (the former Soviet Union) has an array of satellites along with the network of thousands of radars connecting like the US with the command centres—popularly known as Command, Control, Communication and Intelligence (CI-3) encircling the Space, Earth and Sea. The US alone has established the largest communications system in the world. More than 3,000 such networks located in 75 countries are under American CI-3. This military experience of the world led by the US is the most important one for establishing disaster-warning system.[25]

For effective usage of the above communication systems advanced due to the inception of the information technology (IT) in the present world, integral technology to predict the natural disaster like earthquakes in accurate way is the basic one without which effective disaster warning is impossible. Although scientists are skeptical about such accurate prediction, they have been advancing in this field by undertaking series of research work. In fact, Japan had already developed more advanced prediction mechanism by which it could inform the residents of southern California, the US just seconds before earthquake occurred in the 1990s.[26] It is more relevant to understand here, with regard to accurate prediction of earthquake, the pulse of energy generated by the earthquake underneath the earth, which creates primary waves travelling with unprecedented speed.

Due to primary waves and its impact, the secondary waves, are created followed by a cycle of various shock-waves amounting to upward or sideward movements hitting the upper crust violently depending upon the magnitude with which all such wavers are pushed with velocity and destructive capability.[27] Generally, scientists understand shockwaves appearing in the upper crust of the earth by the help of the scientific installations referred above. According to them, the chance of predicting the primary pulse accurately is very remote. However, such accurate prediction on the occurrence of natural disasters, especially the earthquake, may be possible in the future, for which research in remote sensing should be developed by encouraging younger generation[28]. A successful establishments of disaster warning system can very well help the humanity connecting itself through the predominantly available devices such as hand held mobile phones, pagers, televisions, radios, computers, fire/ smoke alarms, and any other type of common communication device.

India has considerable number of remote sensing and communication satellites. Specifically to deal with the natural disaster, the Indian Space Research Organisation (ISRO) has established the Disaster Management Support Programme (DMSP) that helped people during the time of natural disasters like cyclones, landslides, flood, avalanches and tsunamis.[29] It helped collect information about the detail of damages by connecting itself with the aircrafts flying over Tamilnadu and Andaman and Nicobar islands after the tsunami hit these places.

ISRO's National Remote Sensing Agency operating in Hyderabad is playing very important role in advancing technologies relating to remote sensing in India. Therefore, regional disaster management in South Asia can be established with the support of Indian satellites by collaborating with global remote sensing network, especially for effective disaster management in this part of the world.[30] However, it is reported that 70 per cent of the early warning systems established in different parts of the world are false as they are far away from the earthquake prone areas.

Conclusion

Disaster management has become one of the important areas of studies in this present century. As Indian Ocean is the most vulnerable region to such natural disasters including earthquakes and tsunamis apart from being vulnerable to droughts, floods, cyclones, landslides and bush fires, the task for establishing disaster management network has become very significant one in this part of the globe. Therefore, Indian Ocean countries should continue the jobs undertaken in Paris conference held in 2005 for setting up the early warning system in the tsunamigenic places like Java Sumatra and Makaran. For the purpose, they should tirelessly work for establishing links with gigantic communication network of the world community available with more than seventy-five countries now irrespective of politics and cultural differences. Such 'global network' may help the scientists advance further in this field especially predicting the 'primary pulse' of the earthquakes in the future.

NOTES

1. See W.G. Ernst (edit.), *Earth Systems: Processes and Issues* (Cambridge: Cambridge University Press, 2000), pp. 13–26.
2. *Ibid.*
3. See Dhingras, *The World of Questions and Answers* (Delhi: Dhingra Publishing House, 2003), p. 14.
4. *Ibid.*

5. See Haraldur Sigurdsson, *Melting the Earth: The History of Ideas on Volcanic Eruptions* (New York: Oxford University Press, 1999), pp. 1–8.
6. *Ibid.*
7. See W.G. Ernst (edit.), *Earth Systems: Processes and Issues*, No.1, pp. 13–26.
8. See Haraldur Sigurdsson, *Melting the Earth: The History of Ideas on Volcanic Eruptions*, No. 5, pp. 1–8.
9. *Ibid.*
10. See W.G. Ernst (edit.), *Earth Systems: Processes and Issues*, No.1, p. 26.
11. See *The Hindu* (Chennai), 16 March 2005.
12. *Ibid.*
13. See the http:*//www.tsunami.org/; http://www.pmel.noaa.gov/tsunami-azard/links.html/*
14. *Ibid.*
15. *The Hindu,* 14 March 2005.
16. *Ibid.*
17. *Ibid.*
18. *Ibid.*
19. See the http:*//www.disaster-info.net*
20. *Ibid.*
21. *Ibid.*
22. See http:*//www.pmel.noaa.gov/tsunami-azard/links.html*
23. *Ibid.*
24. See William M. Arkin and Richard Field House, *Nuclear Battle Fields: Global Links in the Arms Race* (Cambridge, Massachusetts: Ballinger Publishing Company, 1985), pp. 72–76.
25. *Ibid.*
26. *Ibid.*
27. See http:*//www.pmel.noaa.gov/tsunami-azard/links.html*
28. *Ibid.*
29. *Ibid.*
30. See the http:*//www.disaster-info.net*

Chapter - 7

Human Development and Knowledge Economy

"In Epics and Puranas our history lies buried. You can open them like book"
— Maxmuller

"See all beings without exception, first in your self and then in Me"
— Lord Krishna

Background

The concept of 'knowledge economy' is as old as the civic society—the organized socio-political civilization. Since the very beginning of the civilization that took shape first in the geographical areas of Indus valley in the East, which was followed by Egypt in the West, Anatolia (Asia Minor) in the North, and Sumeria (Iraq and Iran) in the South, the organized life of primitive man was based on, among other things, economy.[1] Such economic life started in the Indus Valley in the sixth millennium B.C. by Dravidians. These primitive folks settled in and around Baluchistan (Pakistan) had knowledge about construction of break houses, domestication of cattle, cultivation of wheat, and barley. In addition, they had knowledge on copper that was turned out to be the primemover for exchange of goods among people in the later period modestly facilitating the economic transaction leading to value economy.[2] Although the knowledge based economic activities were initiated in the early period, it was not yet capitalized even in this new age of information revolution set by the group of IT experts in Silicon Valley of the United States.

The Dawn of 'Knowledge Age'

Based on the historical notes of human civilization, the economic life of man was started in the beginning itself with the conviction of achieving prosperity and peace. In all the stages of civilization these phenomenal thinking of men on peace and prosperity were instrumental for industrial life that led for human development in various spheres. Since the first step for human prosperity was put by Indus valley-man, it can even be thought that the word industry was derived from the word, Indus. Thus, prosperity oriented life in Indus valley led to the development activities of the humankind based on organized knowledge and, therefore, based on economy. Such organized knowledge of the primitive man and his thinking process leading to the formation of present economic system was started around three natural human demands—hungry, thirsty and sleep.[3] For example, the stockpiling of foodstuff, storing of water and comfort stay are the major quest which were responsible for all sorts of economic and human development from the pastoral stage to settlement stage and from the industrial economy to knowledge economy of today.

In fact, the knowledge economy of primitive men was based on the concerted efforts on fulfilling the human demands through the effective usage of knowledge with the cooperation of other human organs. Mainly three systems of human body contribute for systemic activities: bottom level (leg to hip), middle level (abdomen to solder) and upper level (neck to head). Major organs involved in these stages are legs, hands and head. It should be realized here that because of such categorization of analysis, religious sage, Sankaracharya referred to three concepts: *Baahu-bala* (strength of hands), *Mano-bala* (strength of mind) and *Yoga-bala* (spiritual strength).[4] Thus, leg power, hand power and brainpower are the major sources of energy to be utilized with the motivation of fulfilling the human demands.

The first-two powers, of course with the help of the brain, had led for agriculture as well as industry oriented economic activities. Till the time the industrial revolution had started, the phase of agricultural revolution was much influencing the formation of human society. As a matter of fact, agriculture was discovered for about 10,000 years ago. Before discovering the art of agriculture, man was a migrating animal, who was moving from place to place for gathering food, hunting, fishing, etc. Only around 8000 BC he had learned the art of cultivating the soil and settled down accordingly by forming civic society by establishing villages. The agricultural age dominated the human history of civilization till the period 1650–1750 during when the second phase of human life, industrial revolution, had started in Europe. In less than three hundred years, it had influenced the entire world. In Asia, Japan was the first country to experience the second wave of industrialization.

Industrial revolution had changed the entire life style of mankind making a greater impact on economic activity by setting up the factory, the machine, the new smoke stacks, the new transportation system, the new educational system, communication media, the trade and commerce, the new working class, the new class of industrial entrepreneurs, the new banking system, the new educational system, the new culture and entertainment—the cinema, the radio, the mass media like the newspapers and magazines—beside the towns, cities and the breakdown of the joint family system. The revolution continued helping out the humanity have advanced politics, military, economy, etc. in course of time making the brain of men as supreme power of knowledge for human prosperity by advancing the process of human developments to the unimaginable level especially in the fields of mathematical calculation, forecasting techniques, astronomical research, defence and intelligence leading to the production of superior contributive and interactive devices.

Therefore, automatic manufacturing knowledge helped produce bullock cart to bullet, bow to rocket and Abacus (old version of calculating machine) to electronic super computer of today.[5] Brain, being the centre of all these developments, which is pertinent for the formation of knowledge, establishes a comfortable lead in all the spheres of human economy starting from demand to supply and from production to marketing. In fact, knowledge involves various spheres of importance such as information, facts, data, acquaintance, familiarity, awareness, understanding and comprehension. They are all parts and parcels of the knowledge economy.

Managing the Economy—The Foundation for Technological Society

Since the very beginning of the Indus Valley civilization, technology has been playing a dynamic role, as a product of knowledge, for the economic development and the economy that means primarily financial system, wealth, market, country, nation, cost-cutting measure, cutback and saving, has been playing a similar role for the development of technology. They are, therefore, complementary to each other. Thus, the chemistry of economic and technological prosperities depends upon the property of human knowledge, which helps solve the problems of man in all fronts.[6]

Economic crisis—the base for any crisis of man, generally emerges when the demand and supply are not balanced in an equilibrium way. If one is down or up, the crisis is bound to exist. Of course, the degree of crisis varies depending upon the swing of both the elements. However, for solving such problems, technology helps by improving the supply side with sole aim of fulfilling the demands. Demand, being in the state of permanent expansion, branded to be creative demands, makes the supply side always at low resulting on the technological boom. Especially it happened in agricultural fields through green revolution and in diary and poultry developments through white revolution.

The concerted efforts of scientists all over the world made these fields boom much specifically taking into the consideration of the demands of the people. Today the world is having sufficient stock of foodstuff.[7] India and Mexico had gone through great experiences in these fields. The flows of foodstuff to different countries from one country are much improved due to over production. Many developing countries are receiving such foodstuff from developed countries. For example, the United States exports millions of tons of wheat and milk powder to deserving third world countries every year. At the time of crisis, the help exceeds even the expected range. Example can be drawn from the recent experience from Gujarat where millions of people were forced to undergo the agony of poverty due to earthquake.[8]

As Keynes—one of the greatest economists of the 20th century, noted once that the demands of people could be utilized as incentives for improving the financial position of them that would not only help merely in fulfilling their demands alone but also help them participate in productive process by creating a dynamic structure for both demand and supply.[9] The logic with which he pondered on the state of affair of American economy in the early 20th century had helped the US improve rather have a quantum jump in the production side which in turn looked for establishing multinational companies all over the world by simply studying about the existing demand position of the world countries all over.

As a consequence a very big revolution by demand led economic growth was set by Keynes giving importance to positive demand management which is contrary to supply side economic policy known as the hallmark of the paradigm shift that emphasized the importance of restricting money supply for controlling inflation, popularly known as monetarism.[10] However, monetarism, which implies the importance of controlling money supply, was adopted as a model first by Margaret Thatcher, the then Prime Minister of the UK in 1979 and by the former President of the US, Ronald Regan in the subsequent year. The changed economic policy based on monetarism has led the world for the realization of the stabilization programme and structural adjustment programme (SAP) which envisages managing aggregate demand by cutting government expenditure and making the economy efficient as well as competitive respectively.

After the practical demonstration of his 'depression theory' in the twentieth century in American economy, the American Government has been continuously exploiting the economic situation by effectively employing the Keynes economic philosophy until today. It can even be said that the depression theory of Keynes is remaining as one of the everlasting 'managers' of economic crisis not only in the US but also in the newly poised liberal economy of the present world in a given economic climate.[11] As of the reasons, the effective understanding in managing the crisis especially between demand and supply has given way for the expansion of American economy all over the world by establishing multinational companies (MNCs). All the innovative technologies discovered in different fields have been directed, therefore, to serve the economic quest of the US and sustain it by creating dynamic demands structure in the world.[12]

Technology has become, therefore, part of economy without which prosperity of humankind is unimaginable. There are hundreds of thousands of MNCs, which have been effectively intervening with the latest technologies for its own missions. In fact, the dynamic dichotomy for both development and management of economy is based on the premises of the fast changing economic demands of the civil society of today that results in the boom of technological innovations in the managerial fields of organization, the style of function, administration, execution and supervision. If the world copes up with theses dynamic factors effectively, the technocratic society would take care of managing the economic crisis of the future world.[13]

Silicon Valley— The Way for Knowledge Economy

Knowledge economy has to be built in the twenty first century because of the interest for fulfilling the demands of people, especially the deserving and deprived. The recently ended world food conference held in Rome, Italy, it was advocated that millions of people suffering from hunger should be seriously thought about and placed centrally to address any developmental activities in the world despite of their discipline and subject thrusts. It should be noted here that there are more than 800 million people suffering from hunger in the world. On the other hand, it was recorded that there are millions of tons of food grains excessively stockpiled.[14] Therefore it may be stated that the distribution system is still based on business but not on humanism.

In many third world countries, even the information about the number of povertyridden people is not available. Especially the African and some of the Asian and Caribbean countries are suffering from such syndrome even in the much blown out information age of today. Country like India, one of the best in the IT fields has such problem. For example, it is reported that despite over production and stockpiling of foodgrains, thousands of people are suffering from hunger and hundreds of them die due to this perennial problem. Traditional farmers, rich in their knowledge of cultivation, die unnoticed due to poverty and helplessness.[15] Because of the lack of commitments on gathering information, the third world countries are losing potential human resources. It is important to note that hungry is equivalent to slow death of body including brain.

For eradicating such perennial problems of humankind, the Silicon Valley based Californians of United States of America, including majority of the Indian citizens settled in that part of the world, have provided a great boost to the information and communication sectors by devoting their time and energy for promoting IT all over the world. Millions of scientists are working for the cause of transferring such 'knowledge' to many countries of the world resulting on the boom of computer and related technological produces.[16] In fact, the fast track world in the real sense has only substantiated its meaning and viability only when the computer took the lead in demand hierarchy of the people. It should be noted that computer is only a device that can be utilized in all sorts of the job environment without any prejudice and discrimination unlike many other devices so far discovered. As a reason, it is going to be always much demanded in the future by the humanity of the 21st century.

In the early 1990s during the globalization process was initiated, the world had only several thousand computers. However, today, there are millions of computers spread all over the world setting the trends for fast track economic development.[17] Fast track economy, if explained in a simple way, is nothing but reaching the needy people with needy things on time and before time. This way business can grow complimenting the real growth and development of the human kind.

Peace through Information Technology and the Knowledge Society

Therefore, information technology is for empowering people to cross the digital divide for the cause of developing good infrastructure for themselves. From the prehistoric period to the present one man has been gathering information for the purpose of improving life style. Information is, therefore, welfare oriented. Formal period in respect of gathering and catering information came into existence only when the man became food gatherer. Information on whereabouts food thus become the first stage in the history of information technology which brought in the discovery of fire, tools, plant cultivations, domestication of animals, settlement in villages, wheel and metals like bronze and copper.[18]

The Indus valley civilization (2500 BC – 1500 BC), provides economy centric information' especially on accounting the importance of the information relating to the locations of fertile lands, usable metals, the formation of society ruled by merchants, the natural forces worshipped by people and the first and foremost form of information based on the pictographic script. Similarly, the Vedic Age (1500 BC — 1000 BC) provides information regarding migration of Aryans, the emergence of the tribe— Bharata and distinction of Varnas, — Aryans and Dasas. Epic Age (1000BC–600BC) provides information on the writings of Hinduism and the power of priests in the society. The Age of Hinduism and Transition (600 BC – 322 BC) gives an account on the rigidity of caste system in India, the activities against such system by Mahavira and Buddha and the Alexander's invasion crossing the Indus River.[19]

All other civilizations are also giving the similar accounts of human history that have become the economic assets of the present world. A knowledge society would usher societal transformation and wealth generation by effective usage of historical information drawn from various civilizations. For, the application of multiple technologies and techniques of management should be encouraged and pursued regularly.[20] In support of the knowledge society an order for the protection of intellectual property rights should be established without any discriminatory regulations with the aim of helping out the poor countries in the world, especially in Africa, Latin America and Asia

Importance of Knowledge Management

For achieving knowledge society, it is important to establish, as noted, a system for regulation of world intellectual property rights especially referring to the rights of using information. Although such regulation is formed up, it is not fully devoted to serve the needy and deserving poor countries of the world. Knowledge management, therefore, is considered as an important one in the present world. What is Knowledge Management? Knowledge Management is the conceptualizing of an organization as an integrated knowledge system, and the management of the organization for effective use of that knowledge.

As knowledge refers to human cognitive and innovative processes emphasizing the conceptual integration of different types of knowledge, management of the organization or any entity for the matter refers to effective administration, function, execution and supervision. It is one of the hottest topics in business consulting that helps to meet the challenges of competition in the modern knowledge economy.[21] Also, it provides an effective means to the society, which organizes itself humanizing the modern technology by placing human intellect and motivation at the centre.

However, the concept of knowledge management is very broad in terms that cover basically all the "software" of an organization involving the structured data, patents, programmes and procedures, as well as the more intangible knowledge, and capabilities of the people. It also includes the way an organization functions, communicates, analyses situations, comes up with novel solutions to problems and develops new ways of doing business. It also includes issues of culture, custom, values and skills and its relationships with its suppliers and customers. Thus, it encompasses a very broad range of perspectives engaging with the complexities of human intellectual processes, including tacit knowledge, learning and innovating processes, communication, cultures, values and intangible assets.[22] A proper scheme of knowledge management for the regulation and utilization of the world resources has become the first and foremost one for achieving sustainable and equitable development among world nations that would help achieve peace and prosperity.

Conclusion

For achieving knowledge economy and global peace, it is pertinent to build knowledge society based on new social 'order of equanimity', which would contribute for the development of new civilization and culture that can help establish not only economically prosperous nations but also politically cohesive world. Thus, global knowledge society and national development are part which cannot be separated. Such society can be achieved by implementing all the technological means including the information technology at all levels especially considering the present liberalized economic system of the world. Thus, the power of positive knowledge should be in display for empowerment of people at all levels, not the trifling politics among nations.

NOTES

1. See the Website http:*//www.International/ Knowledge Management News Letter.com*
2. *Ibid.*
3. *Ibid.*
4. Swami Ranganathanandji, "Social Responsibility and Public Administration", *Peace March* (Dharwad), Vol. 2, No. 1, July–August 2000, pp.17–18
5. See *Knowledge Management*, No.1
6. *Ibid.*
7. See, M.S. Swaminathan, 'Fighting Hunger: 'Know-How' to 'Do how', *The Hindu* (Chennai), 23 June 2002.
8. *Ibid.*
9. See B.S. Sahay, *Supply Chain Management in the Twenty-first Century* (New Delhi: McMillan India, 2000)
10. *Ibid.*
11. *Ibid.*
12. See, Gary Hammel, *Leading the Revolution* (New York: Harvard Business School Press, 2000)
13. *Ibid.*
14. M.S. Swaminathan, *Fighting Hungry*, No.7, p. 2.
15. *Ibid.*
16. *Ibid.*
17. See, Brian K. Williams, Stacey C. Sawyer, and Sarah E. Hutchinson (edit.), Using *Information Technology: A Practical Introduction to Computers* and *Communications* (Boston: McGrow Hill, 199[illegible]).
18. *Ibid.*
19. See, Prabir Purkayastha, 'Ancient Civilizations and the Aryan race', *People Democracy* (New Delhi). October 15, 2000, p. 5.
20. See, *The Hindu*, 26 June 2002.
21. See, *Knowledge Management*, No.1
22. *Ibid.*

Chapter - 8

Managing the Global Recession Today

"... this (human) body is a most delicate piece of machinery... The spinning wheel is a machine; a little toothpick is a machine. What I object to is the craze for machinery not machinery as such. The craze is for what they call labour-saving machinery. Men go on 'saving labour' till thousands are without work and thrown on the open streets to die of starvation. I want to see time and labour not for a fraction of mankind but for all. I want the concentration of wealth, not in the hands of a few, but in the hands of all."

—Mahatma Gandhi in *Hind Swaraj*, 1924, p. 7

Background

The American economy, aptly described by the Indian Prime Minister, Dr. Manmohan Singh as 'casino capitalism' built over a period of time after the great depression of 1930s, is once again in the phase of depression.[1] As many view, the economy of the US is a 'war economy' and it promotes war among nations. After the Second World War, the US, which followed isolation policy, started involving in international affairs in a full-fledged manner. As it had considerable lead in the field of nuclear technology, it controlled the scientific resources of the world by using atomic bombs on Hiroshima and Nagasaki in 1945. Immediately after the Second World War, it started proliferating nuclear technology to its friendly countries through 'Atom for Peace' proposal by the former President of the US, Mr. Eisenhower in 1953. After 1953, for about hundred wars were fought by the US with small nations, apart from deploying forward based nuclear missiles in different countries and engaging the former Soviet Union in the game of deterrence during the period of 'cold war' that was ended only in 1989.[2] Nonetheless, it could promote its model of growth and development among nations by means of varieties of economic 'deterrent policies', which led for the present economic globalization among nations.

Origin of the World Economic Crisis

During the period of the Second World War, many economic measures were initiated by the world leaders for managing the economic crisis due to war. In the process, 730 delegates from 44 allied nations gathered at the Mount Washington Hotel in Bretton Woods, New Hampshire to participate in the United Nations Monetary and Financial Conference in July 1944 and at the end of the conference they agreed upon a system, popularly known as Bretton Woods System, which established monetary management through rules for commercial and financial relations among the major industrial states. In addition to setting up a system of rules, institutions and procedures, it also established the International Bank for Reconstruction and Development (IBRD) and International Monetary Fund (IMF).[3] According to Bretton Woods System, each country had an obligation to adopt a monetary policy for maintaining the exchange rate of its currency within a fixed value—plus or minus one per cent—in terms of gold and the ability of the IMF to bridge temporary imbalances of payments. In the face of increasing strain, the system collapsed in 1971 following the US's suspension of convertibility from dollars to gold. This created the unique situation whereby the US dollar became the "reserve currency" for the nation-states which signed the agreement.[4] There was no effective initiative from the world leaders to stop the American influence over world economy. Although the members of Non-aligned Movements (NAM) attempted to establish New International Economic Order (NIEO), they could not effectively encounter both the Bretton

Woods System and the American influence over the world economy. Also, the approaches of 'perestroika'—restructuring the economy, and 'glasnost'—openness in politics unleashed by former Soviet Union led by Michael Gorbachev couldn't play the expected 'counter-balance role' due to domestic politics that led not only to the fall of Soviet Union but also to the fall of 'Berlin Wall', the 'cold war', the 'military deterrence', and the 'Balance of power system' resulting in the unification of Europe—the starting ground for cold war politics and, therefore, creating yet another new economic situation in the world.[5] In this connection, the emerging China—the biggest communist country of the present world, having accepted the entry of American economy due to the 'open-door policy' of the Nixon Government in 1972— couldn't do much except its contribution in the field of 'economic zone'. Also, the European nations—especially the UK, Germany and France, considerably engaging in the 'new process of unification', specially after the fall of Soviet Union and 'Berlin Wall', could not allot considerable time for mitigating the economic crisis, specially for regulating the American influence.[6]

As a result, the US had overstretched for its economic ambition by promoting 'uni-polar' approaches and managed to handle almost all the issues of the world community in a single-handed way by violating international norms. In the process, it entered into Afghanistan, Iraq and now in Iran, Syria and Pakistan and wasted huge amount of money. Such involvements had impact in the domestic front and drained the economy considerably. According to report, more than 15 trillion dollars were spent by the US for war-making. It should be noted here that the US is the largest debtor countries in the world.[7] Thus, the American economic-philosophy has been constantly promoting war among nations by creating a 'vicious cycle of violence' in the field of world politics and economics forcing other nations too follow the same methods. Therefore, the 'real economy'—domestic or 'people oriented economy'—couldn't receive much attention either by the local or by the world economists probably with the belief that the changes occurring from above could have 'trickle-down effect' resulting in improving the pace of development locally.

Global Recession and the Road Ahead

Global recession has been in continuous vogue from various period of time due to what one calls it as 'bubble economy' Bubble economy is nothing but believing on creating continuous profit by any means so as to accumulate wealth in constant mode This is what the modern capitalism taught to the world. In this connection, Adam Smith in his book *Wealth of Nation* published in 1776 tinted 'the invisible hand' in reference to the role of state. According to him the state should protect society, individual and provide public good. If it does, people oriented economy will emerge making people as defenders of state economy. In the similar way, the modern economist, Johan Maynard Keynes argued in 1936 for state intervention to attain economic stability. Otherwise, the modern economy based on market forces will fail without seeing the light of equity, trickle down effect, as noted by him will never occur as it should be and IMF/ WB errected on the basis of leissez faire will lead the unilateral free trade to the point of collapse from where return to normal condition will take considerable period of time. Thus, the accumulation of wealth gets into trouble periodically due to ineffective financial system. This economic trend was explained by J.K.Galbraith, an eminent economist who was like Keynes identified the instability of modern capitalism in terms of the drive to accumulative excessive wealth and the fragile nature of the financial system, as follows: "all stock market bubbles exhibit seemingly imaginative, currently lucrative, and eventually disastrous innovation in financial structure"[8] The bubble economy believing on speculative bubble continuously collapsed in various period of times. Such episodes can be noted as follows: the South sea bubble in the early 1700s: the Mississippi bubble, which caused a stock market crash in 18th century France; the Florida real estate bubble in 1920s; the stock market crash of 1929 and in 1987; the Nikkei bubble which began in 1991 and the NASDAQ bubble of 2000. These episodes share a theme, as explained by Galbraith in his book titled 'Money': "a perceived fundamental change in the economy arouses euphoria and heightened expectations of return leading to excess, fraud and collapse... Heightened expectation stimulates a credit boom with the banking system keen to cash in on the new situation... the banks, needless to say, provided the money that financed the speculation that in each case preceded the crash".[9] Similarly, with reference to the present crisis of the world economy, Prime Minister Manmohan Singh pointed out in the recently held Asia-Europe Meeting (ASEM) in October 2008 that a "collective international effort to the international financial crisis must involve infrastructure investments in developing countries as a 'counter-cyclical device' as well as the creation of a Global Monitoring Authority (GMA) to promote global supervision of the world economy". He said further that globalization without the structure of global financial governance had led to severe problems and, therefore, there has been a massive failure of regulatory and supervisory powers. As a result, "speculators have had a free run for far too long a period" and the international institutions like the IMF couldn't do much in this respect watching helplessly the unacceptable failure of effective multilateral supervision of major developed economies and in particular of what has been going on in their own financial markets.[10] It is well known that the US did not bother much about its real economy as it was too much involved in money making from foreign countries. Since its economic plan had been always based on deficit budget, it never had economic sufficiency in this process and, therefore, it had established hundreds of thousand multinational companies all over the world. Without serious involvement in studying its own 'domestic demand and supply dynamics', such a 'super-structural economic plan' was initiated by the US especially for managing the first depression during the 1930s by advantageously using the economic theory of Keynes.

A renowned Indian Professor of economics Prabhat Patnaik, who made a presentation at the UN General Assembly on 30th October 2008, as a member of the Interactive Panel of the UNGA on the Global Financial Crisis, explains:[11] "John Maynard Keynes, writing during the Great Depression, had suggested an alternative stimulus, namely, a comprehensive "socialization" of investment, whereby the state acting on behalf of society always ensured a level of investment in the economy, and hence a level of aggregate demand that was adequate for full employment. This entailed not only a jettisoning of the free market system in favour of state intervention, but also restraints on the free global mobility of finance, since meaningful state intervention could not be undertaken if the nation-state faced internationally-mobile capital." According to him, the Keynesian stimulus was adopted in the post-war period, during what has been called the "Golden Age of Capitalism." However, the process of globalization, involving above all the globalization of finance, which began during the period of Keynesian demand management itself, put an end to that stimulus, and removed a host of regulatory measures that characterized the Keynesian regime. As a result, boosts to aggregate demand has come now increasingly from the stimulation of private expenditure, associated with the creation of bubbles in asset prices, rather than from an adjustment of public expenditure within the context of reasonably stable asset prices. Therefore, he notes with concern:[12] "Not surprisingly, the frequency of financial crises, associated with bursting of these bubbles, has increased greatly after 1973".

In reference to current crisis, he notes further:[13] "The current crisis underscores the need for a new stimulus. Till now, governments have only injected liquidity into the system for stemming the crisis. They initially planned to do so by purchasing "toxic" securities, but eventually had to inject liquidity again equity, through part-nationalization of financial institutions.... But such injection is not enough. Credit does not start flowing simply because banks can access more liquidity; there has to be adequate demand for credit for viable projects by solvent borrowers. This is absent." However, such economic involvement, during the period of world war, was so advantageous and the US, therefore, decided to prolong the same for some more period of time by manipulative economic policies time and again. As planned, the economy of US could manage till 2001 without much trouble. Some believe, if the coldwar could have been prolonged, the American economy would have been safe and continued in the same vine of exploitation.

As of the reasons, the escape route for the present crisis appears to be too far. In this connection the RBI Governor, D. Subba Rao notes that the "global downturn may be deeper, and the recovery longer than expected earlier".[14] According to him, the central task for the conduct of monetary policy has become more complex than before, with increasing priority being given to financial stability. Therefore, the current challenge, as he notes, has to strike an optimal balance between preserving financial stability, maintaining 'price stability', 'anchoring inflation' and 'sustaining the growth' momentum.[15] All these tasks will take time. However, efforts should be made to address the real economy more seriously than ever before and solutions should be found accordingly in four important contexts: free flow credits; support to the most poorest nations; decisive public policies and smart regulations; addressing the underlying challenges of the current financial crisis— massive global poverty, growing social inequality, rising informality and precarious work relating to the process and issues of globalization.[16]

In this context the US President Barack Obama, after meeting with some of the country's economic experts, warned on 8 November 2008 that "the Americans face the challenge of a lifetime...It is not going to be easy for us to dig ourselves out of the hole that we are in....The number one priority is to get Congress to approve an economic stimulus plan that would extend jobless benefits, send food aid to the poor, and spend tens of billions of dollars on public works projects. . . . Effort to unlock the frozen credit and stabilize financial markets,... protecting taxpayers, helping home owners, and not unduly rewarding the management of financial firms that are receiving government assistance….We are facing the greatest economic challenge of our time, and we are going to act swiftly.…I don't underestimate the enormity of the task that lies ahead".[17] In support of his view, the recently published World Bank report titled 'Reshaping Economic Geography' also stresses for a growth based on inclusive economy, economic integration at the local and regional and international levels, which are so far not well balanced.[18]

Thus, the local economy has become now the centre of attraction, which will help for establishing an order for stable and sustainable growth and development at the global level. Such an inclusive development for minimizing present global economic crisis was also highlighted in the G-20 summit held in Washington on 15 November 2008, which was attended by the developed and emerging countries, including India.[19] For immediate effect in this respect, it is necessary to protect the emerging economies of the world like Brazil, Russia, India and China, known as BRIC countries, as early as possible. Otherwise, situation will worsen further creating yet another cycle of crisis. In this context, it is necessary to mention the report of the World Bank. According to it, the expected growth in developing countries will be 4.5 per cent next year instead of the projected growth rate of 6.4 per cent resulting in increasing the number of poverty ridden people. As pointed out by the report, there will be 20 million people further slipping into poverty due to economic recession. This, it added, would be in addition to the 100 million pushed below the poverty line by the sharp increase in food and energy prices over the past two years. For avoiding such development, the World Bank promises 100 billion dollars to poor nations in three years.[20]

Gandhian Alternatives for Present Crisis

Gandhian '*Hind Swaraj*' perspective was originated in 1908 during Gandhiji's return voyage from London to South Africa in answer to the people who believed in the practice of violence for attaining freedom in India and in South Africa published serially in the columns—'to the reader' of the '*Indian Opinion*' edited by Mahatma Gandhi. It was developed into a booklet and turned out to be the first book of Mahatma Gandhi later. It teaches the gospel of love in place of hate and replaces violence with self sacrifice. Referring to its origin Gandhiji stated that the booklet is a result of faithful record of conversations he had with workers, one of whom was an avowed anarchist. It should be noted that during that period of time there were many to oppose '*Hind Swaraj*', also known as 'Home Rule' of Mahatma Gandhi.[21] In fact, the Bombay government banned the booklet. The opponents argued that Gandhi's views were severe condemnations of 'modern civilization'. However, Gandhiji held his views in 1921 that his conviction was deeper than ever before and advocated that India could discard modern civilization. Explaining the core meaning of '*swaraj*', he said:[22] "Do you think that it is necessary to drive away the English, if we get all we want?...We want English rule without English. Is it right? Then it is 'Englishtan' not Hindustan/ *Hind Swaraj*?

Referring to the real civilization. he noted:[23] "I believe that the civilization India has evolved is not to be beaten in the world. Nothing can equal the seed sown by ancestors. Rome went, Greece shared the same fate; the might of the Pharaohs was broken; Japan has become Westernized; of China nothing can be said; but India is still, somehow or other, sound at the foundation. The people of Europe learn their lessons from the writings of the men of Greece or Rome, which exist no longer in their former glory. In trying to learn from them, the Europeans imagine that they will avoid the mistakes of Greece and Rome. Such is their pitiable condition. In the midst of all this, India remains immovable and that is her glory. It is a charge against

India that her people are so uncivilized, ignorant and stolid, that it is not possible to induce them to adopt any changes. It is a charge really against our merit what we have tested and found true on the anvil of experience, we dare not change. Many thrust their advice upon India, and she remains steady. This is her beauty; it is the sheet anchor of our hope." And he continued that "civilization is that mode of conduct which points out to man the path of duty. Performance of duty and observance of morality are convertible terms. To observe morality is to attain mastery over our mind and our passions. So doing, we know ourselves. The Gujarati equivalent for civilization means "good conduct".[24]

In continuation of his advocacy for a new approach for civilization, Gandhi noted further, especially with respect to stable economy as follows: "we notice that mind is a restless bird; the more it gets the more it wants, and still remains unsatisfied. The more we indulge our passions the more unbridled they become. Our ancestors, therefore, set a limit to our indulgences. They saw that happiness was largely a mental condition... I would certainly advise you and those like you who love the motherland to go into the interior that has yet been not polluted by the railways and to live there for six months; you might then be patriotic and speak of Home Rule."[25] In the conclusion of his first book—*The Hind Swaraj*, he notes: "Indian civilization is the best and the European is a nine days' wonder. Such ephemeral civilizations have often come and gone and will continue to do so....I will take the liberty of repeating: (1) Real home-rule is self-rule or self-control; (2) The way to it is passive resistance: that is soul-force or love-force; (3) In order to exert this force, *swadeshi* in every sense is necessary; (4) What we want to do should be done, not because we object to English or because we want to retaliate but because it is our duty to do so."[26] Thus, Mahatma Gandhi's book—*Hind Swaraj* remains very relevant, which can provide alternative solutions for effective management of the economic crisis of the present world.

Gandhian economic plan is based on 'holistic paradigm' and ethical values like truth, non-violence, non-stealing, non-possession, *brahmacharya*, self-suffciency, co-operation, decentralization, equality, bread labour, *swadeshi* and trusteeship, whereas the modern economic plan—Bretton Woods System, is on 'fragmented paradigm'. The present economic plans of the world are mainly influenced by two schools of thought—capitalism and communism. Both have failed to provide better economic order and, therefore, alternative economic order is needed today. Since, the present Bretton Woods model could only help the western economies, poverty among world nations have become the most worrisome phenomenon and almost all the governments of the world nations irrespective of their ideological ramifications act in favour of 'haves' and their plans give much priority to 'ends'. According to Gandhiji, if 'means' are not given priority, whatever achieved by the world will be temporary. Although, the globalization process sway the world, many experts on sustainable economy notes with concern that Gandhian economic solution will be the ultimate one for the present humanity, which encounters the vicious cycle of 'global greed-economy'.

In this context, V.K.R.V. Rao states:[27] "Gandhi's ideas are beginning to command increasing attention in the world that is disillusioned by the working of both capitalism and communism and attracted by the possibility that the circle can be squared with economic growth, social justice, full employment, economic and social equality, political democracy and individual freedoms forming components of a harmonious new social order". Similarly, the western economist, Paul Samuelson, aptly sums up the situation, "under capitalism, it is a case of man exploiting man. Under socialism, it is a case of vice versa".[28]

As the precepts of 'non-violence' and 'tolerance' have deeply infused India's civilization and the great philosophical traditions that emerged from India, including Buddhism preached these basic truths as essential for mankind's progress, India should not deviate from such tradition and it should accordingly adopt the 'holistic paradigm' for alleviating poverty in general and rural poverty in particular. Gandhiji noted: "A votery of *swadeshi* will carefully study his environment and try to help his neighbours wherever possible by giving preference to local manufacturers, even if they are of an inferior grade or dearer in price than things manufactured elsewhere. He will try to remove their defects, but will not, because of their defects give them up in favour of foreign manufacturers".[29] According to Gandhiji, village economy is central one for the development of India. Such economic development will be, as he noted, sustainable leading further for establishing conducive atmosphere for forming a comprehensive 'non-violent economic model.'

In this connection, Mahatma Gandhi pointed out: " In this structure composed of innumerable villages there will be ever widening, never ascending circles. Life will not be a pyramid with the apex sustained by bottom. But, it will be an oceanic circle whose centre will be the idividual, always ready to perish for the village, the latter ready to perish for the circle of villages, till at last the whole becomes one life composed of individuals, never aggressive in their arrogance but ever humble, sharing the majesty of the oceanic circle of which they are integral units. Therefore, the outermost circumference will not wield power to crush the inner circle but give strength to all within and derive its own from the centre".[30] Such model of development should be evolved from the point of view of a 'common' or 'poorest of the poor' who is in a 'poorest village'. For Gandhiji, every economic plan of India should consider the 'last man' and put him in the centre of plan. The benefit should be decentralized in a way comparing neighbours and accordingly 'satisfying the need not the greed' of everyone.

Critical Views on Modern Economy

In debating against modern economy, Prime Minister Vladimir Putin critically noted in his address delivered at a meeting of the Shanghai Cooperation Organisation (SCO) recently in Kazakhstan capital, Astana. He stated that the world has entered a momentous transition towards a multi-polar financial and economic system and, therefore, the Bretton Woods System formed by few countries cannot be allowed to monopolize further the global finances.[31] Modern economy, as noted above, is based upon a fragmentary paradigm. As India is swayed by globalization, it is put in a new world economic environment wherein the cost cutting and competitiveness hold the key to success. Also, there have been diferent approaches to growth—export growth, labour intensive growth and focus on service sector which is now leading. The private sectors were chosen as engines of growth by the government. However, it is important to note that the private sectors will concentrate only on profits rather than generating more jobs for unemployed people.[32]

Moreover, the government has set already a task force on job creation, which is not very successful. It should also be mentioned that since the agriculture, plantation and manufacturing sectors have accommodated more machines in respective fields, the government could not generate 30 million jobs in the Tenth Plan period. So far as the industries are concerned, industrialists want the government to do away from the labour law which are not, according to them, matching the existing order of globalization especially considering on competition. As a matter of fact, reforms and growth have become unfortunately the anti-thesis of labour and employments in the era of liberalization and gobalization.[33]

Moreover, the trend is not encouraging as the public sectors are freezing employment and wages. The task force should, therefore, make an arrangment for creating more jobs not only in urban areas but also in rural areas by encouraging investment of both public and private sectors in respective places. For, innovative plans should be divised and new avenues for investment should also be explored so as to make the benefits to reach common people. The fruit of globalization should be shared in equitable ways by utilising all the modern paradigms that emerges from the global economic settings. In the food sector, India had a plan to feed the entire population with sufficient foodstuff there by making India hunger free by August 15, 2007 as required by UNMDG.

For attaining such goal, the Indian government had adopted the following measures: taking care of the pregnant and nursing mothers, infants and pre-school children, youth, adult, old and infirm persons in the rural areas in particular; developing community food Banks; promoting National Food Guarantee Scheme(NFGS); sustaining and strengthening agricultural progress and management of changes especially in reference to technology, ecology and trade; implementing Grain Bank Scheme (GBS) in tribal areas and 'Sampoorna Gramin Rozgar Yojana'—food for work. All such initiatives are yet to be implemented effectively for the benefit of the rural people.[34] The recent initiatives for involving private sectors in power and transportation fields are also not successful in relation to the development of village power and roads, since the private sectors are interested in 'profit making projects' in urban areas.

It is important to understand about certain basic areas in which all the governments have failed in implementation. For instance, the sanitation sector can be noted. According to the UNICEF and WHO, India faces a large sanitation deficit.[35] At present 1.2 billion people worldwide defecate in the open and India leads with 665 million people as per the 2006 calculation. The journal, *Economist* notes that about 1,000 children die of diarrhoeal sickness everyday in India and to avoid such trends the Government of India planned to construct 103.5 million toilets in individual households by 2007, however, it could only construct 29.9 million toilets during the period of Eleventh Plan and the rest will be constructed only by 2012. In addition, Ballpark estimates that 33,200 million litres of sewage are produced daily in cities of India and only 18 per cent of them are treated and, therefore, it notes further that sanitation in slums in India is unthinkable.[36]

As of the reason, India stands 126 in the human development index, rising inequalities among people. Few people are rich and majority in misery. There are reportedly fourth largest number of dollar billionaires available in India. Whereas around 837 million live on less than rupees 20 a day. Without realizing such an uneven development, the government continue to neglect certain sectors like water, sanitation, education and health and it has reduced the expenditure in welfare sectors. It also reduces the subsidies and life support expenses for poor people while increasing subsidies to the rich and extending unnecessary support for privatization process from intellect to soul. More importantly it also rises the corporate power across the world in an unparalleled way and impose the user fee on everything in ways the poor could not afford.[37] Such contradictory development can be avoided by Indian planners by effectively utilizing the 'treasury of non-violent knowledge' enriched with 'rays of love and affection' by Mahatma Gandhi.

Towards Real Economy

Therefore, Rural India needs a concerted effort with futuristic vision for avoiding the impact of present global recession. Mahatma Gandhi had such vision for developing India based on his plan. He said: "my imaginary village consists of 1,000 souls. Such a unit can give good account of itself, if it is well organized on the basis of self-sufficiency".[38] According to him, India can only develop when a village economy is transformed and given with complete *swaraj*. All its needs should be fulfilled by itself and wants should be restricted. Only then, *gram swaraj*, as desired by him, can be attained. In this context, he stated that "My idea of village *swaraj* is that it is a complete republic independent of its neighbours for its own vital wants, and yet dependent for many others in which dependence is a necessity".[39] His idea on the basic framework for *gram swaraj* in paricular and *poorna swaraj* or *sarvodaya* for alleviation of poverty as a whole in India can be summed up as follows:[40]

(i) Every village will grow for its own food crops and cotton for its cloth;
(ii) It will have a land reserve for grazing its cattle, recreation and play ground for children;
(iii) If there is more land available, it will grow useful money crops, excluding *ganja*, tobacco, opium and the like;
(iv) It will maintain a village theatre, school and pulic hall and houses of worship for all;
(v) It will have its own waterworks, ensuring clean water supply. This can be done through well or tanks;
(vi) Education will be compulsory up to the final basic course;
(vii) The village will be so constructed as to lend itself to proper sanitation. It will have cottages with proper light and ventilation;
(viii) Economic resources obtainable in the nearby surroundings will be used as far as possible;
(ix) Basic medical facilities will be made available in the village; and
(x) Economic activities will be organized on a cooperative basis as far as possible.

The above visions of Gandhiji are put in use in different parts of India in Gandhian Ashrams. For attaining self sufficiency in providing food for all, the leaders of a village should work out on the need of villages and accordingly involve them in cultivation of food crops. Scuh idea is not yet put in use by Indian economic planners, which is one of the basic requirements for eradication of poverty. Although, India claims that it has attained self-sufficiency in food sector, it is not practically done through effective 'public distribution system. As a result, the number of death due to hunger is ever increasing in the villages. It should be mentioned here that due to global slowdown, 44 million new malnourished people are listed by the World Bank in its report published on the 16 October 2008—the World Food Day, which increased the number to 967 million as of now. Also, the report states that by raisinig fund for banking system alone cannot do for removal of poverty. Therefore, effective implementation of policies relating to food for all becomes very important for overcoming the present economic crisis.[40]

In early period, all the villages had some common lands for grazing the cattle, for people recreation and for children play. Today such lands are owned by either by dominant men of villages or by politicians and, therefore, the growing of cattle in villages, especially by poor people are fast vanishing. Since common lands are not available, the villagers cannot grow useful money crops or construct village theatre, schools and public halls and houses of worship for all. It is to be noted with concern that since 1947, the successive governments headed by different political parties neglected villages.[41] Therefore, after even sixty-two years of independence, vital needs of the villages as visualized by Gandhiji such as providing clean water supply, education, sanitation, houses with proper light and ventilation, viable economic resources, basic medical facilities and effective cooperative system for better management of village economy are not attained. Thus, the task of powering rural people has become one of the important tenets for withstanding the present gobal recession trigered by the slowdown of American economy that was formulated from the Bretton Woods system.

Conclusion

India, being one of the leaders of world economy, should play a responsible role by taking advantage from Gandhian principles that are becoming very important in this crisis prone world. Majority of the world leaders, including the American President, Mr. Barack Obama agrees with the relevance of Gandhian principles. Talking to press, Obama stated that Gandhian principle had inspired him.[42] Moreover, the UN is working for spreading 'culture of peace' among nations by realizing Gandhian ideals. To this effect, it has declared this decade (2001–2010) as a 'culture of peace decade' and Gandhi Jayanti Day as the 'International Non-violence-Day'. In such an encouraging international atmoshphere, all like-minded nations along with the support of the UN should work for erecting a new economic order based on 'people centric real economy' by realising *Hind Swaraj* perspectives of Mahatma Gandhi, not for spiralling once again the Bretton Woods System.

NOTES

1. See, *The Hindu* (Chennai), "Manmohan blames it on 'Casino' Capitalism—India moots Global Monitoring Authority for world economy", 25 October 2008, p.1
2. See for more details on Cold War Politics, Robert A. Pollard, *Economics, Security and the Origins of the Cold War, 1945–1950* (New York: Columbia University Press, 1985).
3. See, Kenneth Waltz, *Man, the State and War* (New York: Columbia University Press, 1973 and David P. Calleo and Benjamin M. Rowland, American and World Political Economy Bloomington, Indiana: Indiana University Press, 1973, cited in *http://en.wikepedia. org/ Bretton Woods System)*
4. *Ibid.*
5. See, Robert A. Pollard, *Economics Security and the Origins of the Cold War, 1945-1950*, No.2
6 *Ibid.*
7. See, Kenneth Waltz, *Man, the State and War,* No.3
8. See, *The Hindu*, 16 October 2008, p. 11.
9. *Ibid.*
10. See, *The Hindu*, 25 October 2008, p. 1.
11. *The Hindu,* "The Present Crisis and the Way Forward", 14 November 2008, p. 10.
12. *Ibid.*
13. *Ibid* .
14. *The Hindu,* 25 October 2008, p. 11.
15. *Ibid.*
16. *The Hindu,* Juan Somavia, "Director General of the International

Labour Organization, Time to rescue the real economy, this is not simply a crisis on Wall Street; it is a crisis on all streets," 25 Oct., p. 11.

17. *The Hindu,* "Obama seeks economic stimulus", 9 Nov. 2008, p. 14.
18. *The Hindu,* 14 Nov. 2008, p. 10.
19. *The Hindu,* 16 Nov. 2008, p. 8.
20. *The Hindu,* 13 Nov. 2008, p. 1.
21. See, M. K. Gandhi, *Hind Swaraj or Indian Home Rule* (Ahmedabad: The Navajivan Trust, 1938), pp. 55–56.
22. *Ibid.*
23. *Ibid.*, pp.54–60
24. *Ibid*
25. *Ibid.*
26. *Ibid.*
27. See V.K.R.V. Rao, *Indian Socialism* (ND: Concept Publishing Company, 1982), p. 80.
28. See Paul Samuelson, *Economics* (Auckland: McGraw-Hill, 1980), p. 798.
29. M.K. Gandhi, *Rebuilding Our Villages* (Ahmedabad: Navjivan Publishing House, 1952), pp. 9–98.
30. *Ibid.*
31. See, *The Hindu*, 22 October 2008, p. 15.
32. *The Hindu*, 25 January 2003, For good reading in this aspect, see, Gary Hammel, *Leading the Revolution* (New York: Harvard Business School Press, 2000.
33. *Ibid.*, http://*www.International/KnowledgeManagementNewsLetter.com;* see also, William Stacey, Sawyer and Sarah E. Hutchinson (Eds.), *Using Information Technology: A Practical Introduction to Computers and Communications* (Boston: McGraw Hill, 1999)
34. See, A. K. Sharma, *Rural Poverty in India* (Jaipur: Sublime Publications, 2006), pp. 4–6.
35. *Ibid.*
36. See, *The Hindu*, 20 September 2008.
37. M.K. Gandhi, *Rebuilding Our Villages* (Ahmedabad : Navjivan Publishing. House,1952), pp. 9–98.
38. M.K. Gandhi, *Harijan*, July 26, 1942, p.5; See also M. K. Gandhi, "India of My Dream", *Harijan* (Ahmedabad:Navjivan Publishing House, 1947), p. 100.

39. S.P. Sharma, *Gandhian Holistic Economics* (New Delhi, Concept Publishing Company, 1992), p. 121.
40. See, *The Hindu*, 1 October 2008, p. 18.
41. *Ibid.,* See also *Young India,* June 18, 1931 and Anand T. Hingorani, *The Gospel of Swadeshi (*edi.) (Bombay: Bharatiya Vidya Bhavan, 1976), p. 76.
42. See, *Indian Express* (Chennai), 10, November, 2008.

Bibliography

Primary Sources

United Nations (UN), *An Instructional Guide to Teaching about United Nations* (New York: UN Publication, 1993).

——, *Decades for Eradicating Poverty* 1999-2000 (NY: UNP, 1999).

——, *Economic and Social Commission for Asia and the Pacific* (New York: UN Press, 1979).

——, *World Economic Situation and Prospects* (New Delhi: Academic Foundation on Behalf of the UN, 2008)

United States (US), *Bureau of the Census, International Data Base* (Washington: The Bureau Press, 2000).

Secondary Sources

Book

Hingorani, Anand T. *The Gospel of Swadeshi* (ed.) (Bombay: Bharatiya Vidya Bhavan, 1976).

Rahman, Anisur. *People's Self-Development: Perspectives on Participatory Action Research*,(London: ZED Books, 1993).

Sharma, A. K. *Rural Poverty in India* (Jaipur: Sublime Publication, 2006).

Abdul Kalam, A.P.J. Y.S. Rajan, *India 2020: A Vision for the New Millennium.* (New Delhi: Viking Press, 1998).

Barwell, I.; Edmonds, G.A.; Hower, J. D. G. F.; and de Veen, J., *Intermediate Rural Transport in Developing Countries* (London:Technology Publications, 1985).

Birla Institute of Scientific Research, *India and the Atom* (New Delhi: Allied Publishers, 1982).

Williams, Brian K. Stacey C. Sawyer, and Sarah E. Hutchinson (ed.), *Using Information Technology: A Practical Introduction to Computers and Communications* (Boston: McGraw Hill, 1999)

Gilles, Bretton and Michel Lambert(ed.) *Universities and Globalization: Private Linkages* (Paris: UNESCO Publishing, 2003).

Sahay, B.S. *Supply Chain Management in the Twenty-first Century* (New Delhi: McMillan India, 2000).

Graves Jr., Harvey W. *Nuclear Fuel Management* (New York: John Wiley Press, 1979).

Thomas, Caroline *Global Governance*, Development and Security (Delhi: Pluto Press, 2001).

Center for Development Research, *Panchayati Raj and the Decentralization of Development Planning in West Bengal: A Case Study*(Copenhagen: Neil Webster, CDR Project Paper, 1990).

Smith, Dan *The State of War and Peace Atlas* (London: Penguin Publication, 1997).

Calleo, David P. and Benjamin M. Rowland, *American and World Political Economy* (Bloomington, Indiana: Indiana University Press, 1973).

Dawson, Frank G. *Nuclear Power Development and Management of a Technology* (Seattle: University of Washington Press, 1976).

Dhingras, *The World of Questions and Answers* (Delhi: Dhingra Publishing House, 2003).

Hammel, Gary *Leading the Revolution* (New York: Harvard Business School Press, 2000.

Edmonds, G. C. Donnges and N. Palárca. *Guidelines on Integrated Rural Accessibility Planning*(Manila: ILO/DILG Press,1994).

Sigurdsson, Haraldur *Melting the Earth: The History of Ideas on Volcanic Eruptions* (New York: Oxford University Press, 1999).

Blat, Josef Gold *Arms Control Agreements* (New York: Praeger, 1982).

Payne, Keith. *Laser Weapons in Space Policy and Doctrine* (Boulder: Westveiw Press, 1983).

Waltz, Kenneth. *Man, the State and War* (New York: Columbia University Press, 1973).

Prabha, K. *Terrorism : An Instrument of Foreign Policy* (New Delhi: South Asian Publishers, 2000).

Gandhi, M. K. *Hind Swaraj or Indian Home Rule* (Ahemedabad: The Navajivan Trust, 1938).

——, *Rebuilding Our Villages* (Ahmedabad: Navjivan Publishing House, 1952).

——, *India of My Dream* (Ahmedabad:Navjivan Publishing House, 1947).

Chomsky, Noam *Rouge States* (Mumbai:Indian Research Press, 2001).

Samuelson, Paul *Economics* (Auckland: McGraw-Hill, 1980).

House, Richard Field and William Arkin, *The Nuclear Battle Fields: Global Links in the Arms Race* (Cambridge: Ballinger, 1985).

Pollard, Robert A. *Economics Security and the Origins of the Cold War, 1945-1950* (New York : Columbia University Press, 1985).

Roach, Ruth and Otavio Roth, *Universal Declaration of Human Rights* (New York: UN Press, 1998).

Rocha, Ruth and O. Roth, *Universal Declaration of Human Rights (UDHR)* (New York: UNP, 1998).

Sawyer and Sarah E. Hutchinson (edit.), *Using Information Technology : A Practical Introduction to Computers and Communications* (Boston: McGraw Hill, 1999)

Fan, Shenggen (Ed.) *Public Expenditure, Growth, and Poverty* (New Delhi : Oxford University Press, 2008).

Sinha and Subramanian, *Nuclear Pakistan* (New Delhi : Vision Books, 1980).

Sharma, S.P. *Gandhian Holistic Economics* (New Delhi : Concept Publishing Company, 1992).

Columbus, Theodore A. and James H. Wolfe, *Introduction to International Relations: Power and Justice* (Prentice Hall of India, 1981).

Rao, V.K.R.V. *Indian Socialism* (New Delhi : Concept Publishing Company, 1982).

Ernest, W.G. (ed.), *Earth Systems: Processes and Issues* (Cambridge: Cambridge University Press, 2000).

Arkin, William M. and Richard Field House, *Nuclear Battle Fields: Global Links in the Arms Race* (Cambridge, Massachusetts: Ballinger Publishing Company, 985).

Articles

Amaury de Riencourt, "India and Pakistan in the Shadow of Afghanistan", *Foreign Affairs* (New York), Vol. 62, No. 2, winter, 1982/83, pp.416-417.

Mahadev Horatti, "Peace Message for New Millennium", *Peace March*, Vol.2, No. 9 & 10, September-Oct. 1999, p. 3-14

M. Prabir Purkayastha, 'Ancient Civilizations and the Aryan Race', *People Democracy* (New Delhi) October 15, 2000, p. 5

M. Sivaraman, "World March of Women", *People Democracy*, Vol. 24, No. 46, Nov. 12, 2000, p. 12.

P. Moorthy, "Indus Valley to Silicon Valley: A Study on Knowledge Economy and Global Peace" *Peace March* (Dharwad), Vol.1, No. 5, Oct-Dec. 2002, pp. 24-32.

Parama Sinha Palit, "The Kashmir Policy of the United States: A Study of the Perceptions, Conflicts and Dilemmas". *Strategic Analyses* (New Delhi), Vol. XXV, No. 6, Sept. 2001 pp. 781-783.

Robert Chambers, "The Origins and Practice of Participatory Rural Appraisal", *World Development* (New York), Vol. 22, No. 7, July 1994, pp. 234-42.

M.S, Swaminathan 'Fighting Hunger: 'Know How' to 'Do How', *The Hindu* (Chennai), 23, June 2002, p. 8.

——, "Food, Peace and Development", *The Hindu*, 29 November, 2000, p. 8.

Swami Ranganathanandji, "Social Responsibility and Public Administration", *Peace March* (Dharwad), Vol. 2, No. 1, July-August 2000, pp.17-18.

William Korey, "NGOs: Fifty Years of Advocating Human Rights", Issues of Democracy, *USIA Electronic Journals*, Vol. No. 3, October 1998, pp. 42-52.

Newspapers and Periodicals

Indian Express(Chennai)
National Herald (New Delhi)
Nucleonic Week (New Delhi)
The Hindu (Chennai)
The Pioneer (New Delhi)
Times of India (New Delhi)
United Nations Newsletter (New Delhi)

Webliography

http://www.aleanation.com
http//www.bretton woods system.com
http://www.dallasnews.com
http://www.disaster-info.net
www.EMERGIC org.com
http://www.i-b-r.org
http://www.International
http://www.knowledge management newsletter.com
http://www.health.com
http//www.hri.ca.com
http://www.international.*com*
http//www.ncpa.org
http://www.poverty.com
http://www.pmel.noaa.gov
http//www.terrorism.com
http://www.tsunami-azard
http://www.tsunami.org
http://www.un.org/chronicle
http://en.wikepedia.org
http:// www.world bank.org

Index